Do What N _____

The Purpose Driven Career Transition Guide

By

Katherine Ann Byam, Author,
Sustainability Activist, Consultant & Coach

Do What Matters

Copyright © 2022 By Katherine Ann Byam

All rights reserved.

ISBN: 978-1-7396441-3-0

Contents

Dedication..1

Foreword: From the Author...................................2

Critical Acclaim...7

Prologue – The Aligned Mission............................10
Do-What-Matters-The-Purpose-Driven-Career-
Transition-Guide. 10
The Purpose Driven Career Transition Guide: Chapter
& Section Summaries..16

Introduction: Context and the Case for Change 27
Theme 1 - The Planetary Dimension.......................28
Theme 2 - The Socio - Economic Dimension 36
Theme 3 - Governing the System.............................43

Part 1: Your pathway to self-mastery......................47

CHAPTER 1 - If it's important, build a model –
Creating a conscious self-improvement plan..............48
Some commonly used if not consciously evaluated
mental models...49
Mental models can also form cognitive biases.......52
Developing your Personal Models..........................55

CHAPTER 2 - Who are you, really? - How to begin a
self-discovery journey 57
Who are you really?..57
Mind-Map your way to success.............................67
Capture Flow 69
The cast in your movie 72

CHAPTER 3 - Career Models - Types of career paths to deliver on your purpose..73

Why do you need a job and what purpose does it fulfil in your life?..73

CHAPTER 4 - The Constant Learner - Developing a growth and net-positive mindset 86

The active learning revolution 89

Passive Learning 94

Organisational Unicorns 97

CHAPTER 5 - Your Goals Need Conscious Action - How to take action toward your purpose 99

The Outcome Wheel ™ 100

What's driving your wheel? 102

Identity 105

Beliefs and values 111

When your children define you 112

CHAPTER 6 - The Nine Steps to Positive Impact Career Transitions..**118**

The Nine steps follow a certain logic 119

Part 2: Social, Credible, Responsible - How to become an advocate for change 129

Clarifying your offer to the world 130

CHAPTER 7 - What's the point of your job really? - Why should you do what you do? 132

Does your job matter? 132

Why does your job exist? 134

The Sustainability Conversation 136

Critical Skills 137

CHAPTER 8 - Is it persuasion, influence, or manipulation? - How we get others to follow our lead... 149

What's love got to do with it? 152

CHAPTER 9 - Money and Wealth - What does money have to do with it?..................................161

Let's talk about money...................................161

Wealth...168

CHAPTER 10 - Your Digital Twin - How do you show up credibly and responsibly online?.................171

Online and offline..171

Your network is your net-worth.................173

Key Personal Brand Principles...................174

My Brand Story..175

CHAPTER 11 - Busting HR Myths - Improving the Human Resource Management landscape.................179

My life and HR..179

Recruitment and ATS tracking...................180

Jobs seeking culture fit.................................183

Management vs Leadership 185

Reward structures based on the market.............188

Part 3: Jump, But Know How to Land - "Governing" the first 90 Days 191

CHAPTER 12: Onboarding - Navigating your new job 194

Power dynamics...194

A guideline for constructing your onboarding plan 196

CHAPTER 13: Habits and Contexts 200

Personal systems...200

CHAPTER 14: How to Create the Perfect Pitch........204

What's your pitch? 204

Essentials of a good pitch 205

CHAPTER 15: Better than average, not perfect.......209

Perfection 211

CHAPTER 16: Duds and Explosives..............................217
Things are going to go dark a bit...............218
Narcissists 219
Psychopathy..220
Machiavellianism 223
What about the Duds? 224
Boundaries are your friend 225
The Role of Culture....................................226
Dealing with Fear and Anxiety..................227

CHAPTER 17: Support for your Journey....................233
The leader needs a guide. 233
How to choose a coach, mentor and or
therapist 236

Epilogue - The Aligned Mission.............................240

What's Next in the Series.......................................246
Designed by Diversity, Built by Inclusion 246
The Purposeful Path - The Entrepreneur's guide
to impact and income. 247
The Naked Finger - A single woman's journey to
find herself and her passion......................249

References..252
The First 10 Episodes of Do What Matters 253
The Top 10 Episodes of Where Ideas Launch 253
The Top 10 books that inspired this work 254
The Top 10 movies that form part of the
inspiration for this work. 255
The Top 10 TV series that form part of the
inspiration for this work 255
YouTube videos relevant to this work 256
Websites referenced in this work 257

Acknowledgements 259

About the Author...263

Resources...265

Dedication

I dedicate this book to my parents, Forge and Len, without whom I wouldn't have the foundation I needed to build the career I wanted, several times over on repeat.

I also dedicate it to the next generation, the children of cousins and friends who will next inherit the challenges of creating a sustainable planet from us. May they be stronger than we were and make the tough choices we couldn't. May they bring to life the wellbeing economy they and their children deserve.

This goes to all children, but specifically to my "little sisters" Isabella and Gabriela (UK, Honduras, Dominican Republic), my god son Sage, and all my "niblings" of friends and family around the world; Rinaldo, Mekhi, Kara, Stefan and T'Challa (Trinidad), Emma Z (UK, Spain, Dominican Republic) , Emma L (UK, Australia, Mexico), Che and Zeke (UK and Trinidad), Ethan & Aurora (Trinidad), Domingo and Josefa (Chile & Panama), Julian (Mexico), Nicolas and Eric (Brazil & Malaysia), Arya & Alex (Trinidad) Alejandro and Eduardo (Costa Rica), Benjamin (Venezuela and USA), Violette & Clotilde (France), Kai (Trinidad), Lucas and Uma (Argentina and the Netherlands), Khabeer and Issa (Trinidad).

Foreword:

From the Author

What's your purpose?

For some of us, this question is a deep ache that we spend a lifetime seeking to heal.

For many, our children provide that clear definition of what we exist on earth to do - providing handsomely for them and sustaining a legacy for ourselves through them becomes our *raison d'etre*.

For yet another group, it's about enjoying the present moment ever so fleeting and ever so beautiful.

For still others it can be financial goals, social status, contribution toward an important discovery or transformation, or immortalisation for your work in history.

Maybe you want all of this for yourself, or a few of these pathways call to you, but by the end of this book, I expect you'll be moved by something I've written, and connect more dots with the doubts already percolating in your mind.

I'm not going to guarantee you will be happy with everything you find, when walking on this path. The journey to tapping into that deeper version of self can be as shocking and disturbing as it is illuminating.

When I'm coaching there is no judgement. However, in this book, I'll readily tell you that I'm biased, and I'll make suggestions of things I'd like you to ponder, all coming from the intention of sustaining life of all varieties on Earth.

Whether my words find a home with you or not, I feel relaxed in the comfort you'll find clarity on your path to purpose, and tangible tools to help pave the way for what you are deeply called to do, whatever that may be. The one thing I don't want for you is the avoidance of choice.

The decision about whether you hand over your fate to something outside yourself or go deep within is entirely yours. Yet, I advocate for "happening" to your life, instead of letting it happen to you.

Before you read on, let me be straight. I am not your guru. I'm a self-styled coach, relying as much on personal experiences as on training. I've been called an alchemist by clients, precisely because I integrate all my learning and experiences into the way I see life and decisions. I'm a qualified Neuro Linguistic Programming practitioner and have received formal coaching training during my lengthy career as an employee at multinational companies. I completed an MBA in 2017 and enjoyed 20+ years of corporate experience within the FTSE Top 10, primarily involved in multi-million-pound change programs.

I've travelled extensively for work and collaborated with people from 150 nationalities. I'm also an entrepreneur with aggregated online communities exceeding 15,000 people. I've observed the heck out of everyone and every relationship I've ever had. I became sustainability conscious in 2015.

What I'm about to share with you, may resemble *self-help coaching speak* (yes, I've also read most of the trendy self-help books). Importantly though, it will be practical, multi-layered, and integrated, leveraging as many of the different perspectives needed to illustrate why you in fact have choice.

I've received my best lessons from making transitions; across cultures, teams, borders, languages, and different fields of training, and from being a voracious consumer of critical thought and provocative content throughout my life. It occurred to me that this is what I want most for you too.

I want you to tune in from time to time on whatever is taking place around you and amplify that mostly silent *why* voice in your head. Question everything, more often than you already do - almost how children do. Acknowledge that asking the question won't always get you a satisfactory answer, so keep searching. Suspend judgement where you currently have strongly held views.

Alternate between the *blue pill* and the *red pill* in Matrix parlance. I'm not somehow indirectly advocating for drugs, although there's a lot to be said about the power of psychedelics and psychotropics to ease depression, stress, and anxiety, but that's for another book, too much to unpack there.

Amplifying everything takes all your resources, so I don't recommend it full-time. The task I'm setting for you is to connect with yourself as an active, integral, part of the world around you, and not as an island unto yourself, or the life of the party either. In my experience, real change comes from acknowledging how powerful it is when an entire room dances in a choreography; not always making the same moves, but each move somehow balances out the others. This is what I'd like you to embody as you expand your personal horizons.

Being present is only part of the journey. You are today sitting on a gold mine of experiences you seldom tap into. I'd like you to leverage those for what we are going to create.

There is (dare I say it?) some cosmic magic in extracting insights from your past, linking that to your current experiences and anticipating how you can craft a trajectory to create the future you want.

Eastern philosophies appear to be proving themselves timeless when it comes to connecting with self and with nature. In Japan, as you may already be familiar, they have a word, Ikigai - that describes that for which you are passionate, which the world needs, which you are skilled at, and can be fairly or handsomely paid for. This equation has never been more important and trickier to get perfectly right. It's good that perfect isn't the goal, rather better and closer every day is.

Meditation is also having its time in the spotlight, as science is finally catching up to what the ancients have known all along; research has proven all the ways in which meditation supports stress relief, eases anxiety, and expands the neuroplasticity of our brains, even into our later years. It is also thought to help us with expressing empathy, altruism, and kindness, to self and others.

The key is how we integrate our learning, experiences, and desires into practices that shape and sustain our future.

This book will not just help you find your purpose and ease that ache, it will also pave a path to a more integrated life, developing meaningful connections with the natural environment and societies within which you live.

I have a few resources already available on my website, and more to come if you want to get ahead of the book and dip in there, at www.katherineannbyam.com. Looking forward to being your guide for the next few hours.

You've got this.

Critical Acclaim

❖ *Amazon #1 Best Seller*

On launch day 29th July 2022, Do What Matters – The Purpose Driven Career Guide achieved the number one rank on the Amazon Best Seller charts in the UK. In the weeks around the launch date it also achieved top 10 Best seller spots in the United States, India, and Brazil. In New categories, the book achieved number 1 rankings across multiple categories in the US and in the UK, with top ten positions in India, Germany, Brazil and Canada.

❖ *Archita Sivakumar Fritz, Digital Marketing Executive, Podcaster and Non-Profit Executive*

This book is a revelation in so many ways that I cannot enumerate. Each chapter had me go to places I hadn't considered going; to my experiences, my biases, my joys, and my gifts foremost among them! This book doesn't just recommend what I should consider in my journey to building a net – positive life, it puts the steering wheel in my hand, with a road map and tangible actions to plot out what's meaningful to me! I have lengthy notes. I highly recommend it!

❖ *Kate Davis, Leadership Specialist and NED*

Do what matters is a brilliant resource for anyone looking to upgrade their senior-level career, or even those who need to sense-check their direction in life. Thorough, widely researched and thought provoking, this is a very clever and accessible book taking you from 'what do you really want and why?' to on boarding in your new role and beyond.

Highly recommended.

❖ *Carlos Alberto García: Senior Audit Manager*

"I loved this book! It contains a wealth of information that will guide anyone transitioning career into the right path. It inspired me to transition into a better, purpose driven version of myself. I'm recommending this to colleagues and friends"

❖ *Ludwig May: Director at Core Fundamentals*

Do what matters allows you to join Katherine on her journey of self-discovery over the last several years. I found myself reflecting: why did I not write this myself and how fulfilling would my life have been if I had only read this earlier? As you laugh, cry, and reminisce with her, she invites you to make the choices about your life with intention. Katherine guides you, step by step along a roadmap and provides the tools to allow you to make the impact your world requires right now. Please accept her invitation.

❖ *Melissa Rider Carson: Leadership Coach, Organisational Talent Strategy Advisor*

"If you're at a crossroads in your life, wondering if this is it, it's time to read The Purpose Driven Career Transition Guide. Katherine provides a wealth of ideas and content on how to think about a life that is centred on purpose. She provides great tools, examples, and resources for people to go deeper. She also shares her sources of inspiration, allowing me to dig in deeper where I want to go."

Prologue –

The Aligned Mission

Do-What-Matters-The-Purpose-Driven-Career-Transition-Guide.

Every word in the title of this book holds weight, and each could be its own book. My mission over the next 250 plus pages is to focus on the topic of career transitioning, linking it back to the idea that we are amidst a tremendous groundswell of change, and that you and every living person you care about are either positively or negatively contributing to the eventual outcomes of this movement.

No one is on the fence. Few of us can calculate the carbon, social and governance footprint of all our actions, and those of our families, and it's up to you to decide how you want to act and who you want to be remembered as from this paragraph forward.

We will go into a methodology I use to guide clients through strategic shifts and pivots no matter the goal as the tools can be repurposed for any outcome. How you go about taking action and delivering on your goals will be unique to you, even if it follows a standard structure.

❖ Taking Net-positive action

I am Katherine Ann Byam - a black Caribbean female entrepreneur in the United Kingdom with a mission to have a net-positive impact on the communities I'm in and on the planet in which I live. I am guided more by purpose than by profit and want to help create a world where life is safely preserved.

There is a lot more to unpack in this identity statement. What does Net-positive mean? You can refer here to the book by the same name written by Paul Polman and Andrew Winston, but essentially it means: **does my work help or harm the planet and or society as a whole?**

I set out to write a book that inspires net-positive action by presenting different ideas, scientific truths, and critical inflection points from your own life. My intentions are to help, and to position the work that I do and expertise I have, to support leaders on their journey to deliver the changes the world needs.

Who wants to be a billionaire? I understand the allure of generational wealth. Yet if it means we consume more resources or endanger more lives with our thirst for rapid wealth accumulation, we'll use more than we need to, and disrupt the very future we seek to protect. All the money in the world left for your children without a planet to live on does nothing to help anyone.

Be ambitious. I'm not advocating the end to ambition, but measure your ambition with other metrics too, such as atmospheric regeneration, habitat restoration, well-being index and impact on people within your sphere of influence.

If you want to give your children every privilege, consider an innovative and practical education. Train them to become problem solvers, change makers. *Net-positive* influencers. Give them more options than you've given yourselves. Don't be complicit in their demise.

No system operates without compromises; after all, animals eat animals in the wild, and water, as beautiful as it is, can destroy. You will no doubt continue to face tough calls that sacrifice one thing for another or diminish the potential of both; my only wish is that you do this with clarity of mission, values, and purpose, and with clear intention in your actions.

Every chapter has been infused with the principles of sustainability. Your role as leader has expanded, as much as it has changed, as we go forward into this new era.

If I could convince you of one thing, it would be that you have power, in any career situation you happen to be in. With that knowledge and some new skills at analysing situations, I hope to help you raise your consciousness and make better and more aligned decisions, seeing around the corners at every horizon.

❖ Sustainable Innovation

As an Entrepreneur, I spend much of my time with a community of over 4,000 women in sustainable business on Facebook, more than 6,000 professionals on LinkedIn and over 3,000 connections on Instagram, talking about all the ways we can do better business.

I developed a method I call Green *Idea to CEO*, – a concept borne out in Season 3 of *Where ideas launch – The Sustainable Innovation Podcast*, talking about the precise ways in which we can innovate business models, products, and methods of marketing to create businesses that earn revenue and generate positive impact. These principles apply to your corporate roles too.

"Abundance is a lie in our current context, but it doesn't have to be. We can all thrive on this planet, but it's going to need us to rethink how we design our lives and the way we extract resources from her without damaging her future output demands."

I got started in earnest on my sustainability journey in a classroom in Grenoble, France, in 2015. The topic was innovation, and jugaad or frugal innovation to be precise. And the principles of frugal innovation were not actually foreign to me.

My mother practiced them all her life. In fact, so much of who she was, and still is, has become more precious to me as I navigate and build my services to support sustainable and impact-driven leaders like myself.

Businesses continuously design innovative solutions for products that come with an increase in price, but not always with an increase in value. We've built an economic machine that's designed to make a few rich, and others, to keep them rich, without much regard for the majority.

In some countries, we don't really have a history of doing business any better. We moved from the property of the crown to the property of the Lords and Ladies to the property of the privateers, pirates and the independent landowners that arose after the "New World" was discovered.

Yet there are examples of designing social systems that work for business and society, that are well worth exploring before you decide on how you commit to this in your new role or venture.

❖ The Triple Bottom Line

There is a great buzz around **people, purpose, and planet**, for a reason, and it has implications for your personal and business growth goals.

Let's tackle a few questions first; What does sustainability mean? And what does it have to do with your purpose and career transition?

Sustainability is the ability to operate existing systems without degradation or loss, and most importantly without compromising future generations.

As you would expect, this book focuses on how to choreograph your next move, but as an activist for the cause of saving our home planet, I'd like to show you why I believe sustainability is an essential precursor to what you do next.

Before we begin the career transition specific elements of the book, I invite you to join me in exploring three themes. These themes are the precursor to everything that this book promotes. They will support your knowledge and understanding and broaden your choices when taking action in your career or business toward the *net-positive* impact that you want to have. The themes are summarised here, with more detail to follow.

Theme 1 - The Planetary Dimension

Whether you believe that God made the earth in 6 days and rested on the 7th, avidly follow the geological and astronomical records, or you've seen the brilliant engineering that is the James Webb Space Telescope, you'll acknowledge that our lives are miracles. The number of things that needed to come together perfectly for us to not only exist, but to be sentient, thinking, creative and innovative beings is a gift we've been given. Long may we be able to use that gift in the pursuit of our own longevity as a species, and in the new versions we will create of our world to come. In this section we explore planetary sciences to learn what these can teach us about how we do business.

Theme 2 - The Socio - Economic Dimension

To enjoy the fruits of our labour, we need more people to prosper. Yet, how we measure prosperity also needs a new story. We have long used GDP as a measure for how we create opportunity and demonstrate growth, but today we have a mandate for a new metric, wellbeing. In this theme we get into the social dimensions of the new world we ought to create.

Theme 3 - Governing the System

At the time of writing, many long-established democracies are battling through leadership and governance struggles. The US, the UK, and France to name a few. Without systems of governance, development slows, or reverses altogether. In this theme, we consider what is needed to make change happen, and then make it count. We look at systems of governance to support a 1.5-degree Celsius warmed earth.

The themes within *The Aligned Mission* concept will become integral to the way you make decisions if you let it. Leverage this learning for the greater good.

The Purpose Driven Career Transition Guide: Chapter & Section Summaries

❖ *Part 1 - Your Environment and You*

Your pathway to self-mastery.

"Struggle does not come from winning. Your struggles develop your strengths. When you go through hardships and decide not to surrender, that is strength." - Mahatma Gandhi

We know it theoretically, but often we don't live in the knowledge that the change, and the growth we seek must start with ourselves. If you reflect on the best leaders you've experienced in your lifetime, there are likely common themes that appeal to you. Whether it be strength, conviction, calm, anticipation, persuasion, confidence, openness or vulnerability, *Self-Mastery* is the journey that helps great leaders deliver on their potential. Whether you think you want to be a leader or not, your personal achievements in life align to your leadership ability, even in the context of leading self. This is where our journey begins.

Chapter 1 – *If it's important, build a model*

Creating a conscious self-improvement plan.

In this chapter, we discuss the significance of models on how we do anything. We explore when modelling is helpful in giving structure, and when models take us so far down the wrong path that we struggle to recover. Whether you realise it or not, you have many operating models running your life, that if you acknowledge you can improve. You also have some models that are absolutely best in class and carry much of the responsibility for your repeated successes. The key is knowing which is which!

Chapter 2 – *Who are you, really?*

How to begin a self-discovery journey.

In this chapter we explore self-discovery through two lived examples, my own, and a guest of both my podcasts, to help you draw some tools and inferences as to how you step into the person you feel completely in alignment with. This section uses storytelling and thinking prompts, jot a few thoughts down on a notepad as you go through it as you may want to revisit them later on.

Chapter 3 - *Career Models*

Types of career paths to deliver on your purpose.

In this chapter we discussed nine different approaches we can take to fulfilling what we want to achieve from a career. Whether it be purpose, challenge, fulfilment, income, or other, it's healthy to not just follow traditional conventions and think more broadly about different ways to fulfil these goals.

Chapter 4 – The Constant Learner

Developing a growth and *net-positive* mindset.

Shake up your learning habits. In this chapter we discuss the importance of being a continuous learner, and some of the structured and unstructured ways to pull this off; both are exceedingly important to my process as an example. I'm always learning, even when I'm playing. The conversations I have with guests on my podcast are some of my most important sources of social learning. Stay present to the lesson wherever it comes from. Have an early example of implementation, so you can figure out how to integrate new ideas into what you do every day.

Chapter 5 - Your Goals Need Conscious Action

How to take action toward your purpose.

In this section we discuss the Outcome Wheel (™) and how to use it to evaluate your life and its decisions. In the book Atomic Habits by James Clear, he speaks at length about how to integrate new behaviours and actions toward your personal development. I recommend his work and I recommend using the Outcome Wheel ™ to frame the ways in which different characteristics of who you are today, drive who you will become tomorrow.

There is one external driving force that appears stronger than any other, which is your children (up to a certain age anyway) so we are going to examine the influence of their lives on your choices.

Chapter 6 - The Nine Steps to Positive Impact Career Transitions

In this chapter we discuss the *Nine Step Model* which was conceptualised before the COVID19 pandemic, but really gained traction and shape as I interviewed and surveyed friends and budding entrepreneurs impacted by the crisis. I've been using this model since mid-2020 with clients and friends with remarkable success over the last 2 years.

These nine steps are spread out and covered in more detail throughout the remainder of this book.

- Map out Where You Are
- Succession Planning
- Next Role Planning
- Strategy, Social Media, Network
- Digital Brand Building
- Systems and Trends in Your Industry
- Onboarding & Stakeholders
- Your Own Systems
- Pitching Your Ideas for the New Chapter

❖ *Part 2 - Social, Credible, Responsible - How to become an advocate for change.*

This section takes us from an intense focus on self in part 1, to reflecting that version of self in the context of others and what you have to offer the world.

The actions needed from this section are more social and brand based, with a heavy dose of authenticity, ethics, and responsibility on top. If you've got clarity on who you are and what you want, you can work with a branding expert to help you put those ideas and values into colours, images, perspectives, texts, and icons that become part of what others associate you with. This is valid whether you are an employee in the traditional sense, or a freelancer or contractor. In this age of remote work and 4-day work weeks, the concept of personal branding becomes even more pertinent, as people need a variety of ways to build trust with you. As we move increasingly virtual and integrate the metaverse into our day to day, a brand identity and even an avatar goes a long way for memorability and networking.

Chapter 7 – What's the point of your job really?

Why should you do what you do?

Here we explore six ways to evaluate the rationale behind your job. We also dig into the skills that are needed universally across all jobs but are not necessarily present and well developed in all job candidates, contractors, and freelancers. We then integrate sustainability into your job roles to assess the impact. It would be useful to sit with your current job, or the next one you plan to do, and see how you can apply these concepts for your situation and context after soaking in this material.

Chapter 8 – Is it persuasion, influence, or manipulation?

How we get others to follow our lead.

In this chapter, we discuss an area of both beauty and complexity. To make things happen, and create momentum for change, you need to influence others. To crack this ethical tightrope, it's helpful to understand that free will and choice don't exist without a context, in our current social construct of human civilisation. If we value "civilisation", we need to have some shared values and shared meaning with others which comes at some cost to personal freedom. Let's explore persuasion, influence, and manipulation, and experience this three-headed animal from a few different perspectives.

Chapter 9 - Money and Wealth

What does money have to do with it?

There's so much destructive advice about money and wealth accumulation that I decided to dedicate a chapter to understanding how it works, why it matters and how other forms and substitutes for money are gaining prevalence. This chapter dives into the depths of money so we can make more sense of what is fed to us at scale.

Chapter 10 - Your Digital Twin

How do you show up credibly and responsibly online?

Digital twins are buzzwords at the moment but represent a useful way to frame creating your own personal brand footprint in the online space. We talk about how to build and contribute to communities and show up for the values and ideas you want to represent.

Chapter 11 - Busting HR Myths

Improving the Human Resource Management landscape.

For leaders of businesses, employees, freelancers, coaches, contractors, and consultants, it's useful to understand the lay of the land when it comes to HR in organisations, because there are so many opportunities there to drive change, inclusion, and fairness. It's so ripe for change, it's difficult to ignore so I've dedicated this chapter to getting into the underbelly of the human capital conversation.

❖ Part 3 - Jump, But Know How to Land

The First 90 Days.

For some, this is where the career strategy begins. There's no denying that this is fundamental and needs strategy. Developing that strategy without the two sections that came before, is a recipe for painfully sustaining business as usual toward some dangerous consequences.

The landscape of business has changed since Michael Watkins first wrote his famous bestselling text "The First 90 Days". The good news is that we are problem solvers. We are people who are armed with tools, mental models, and frameworks to break down the problems facing businesses in becoming more responsible actors while still profit seeking. We are emotionally intelligent and more versed on complexity than we have been before.

Chapter 12- Onboarding

Navigating your new job.

Onboarding is less about technical skills and competence, and more about understanding where power flows and how decisions are made in your new context. You won't find those subtleties following the corporate induction programme, you are going to need to craft your own plans on how to access what's happening below the surface in your new reality. This chapter provides guidance for strategizing insights during your first 30 days. Here's how to get it done.

Chapter 13 - Habits and Contexts

Creating a compelling personal playbook.

How you do anything is how you do everything. At least so I've heard and hope it's not true! But there is some merit to it, and a lot of merit in learning how to continuously improve what you do every day by creating a personal playbook. This chapter covers the foundations of habits and provides references for going on to learn more about enhancing your skills as well.

Chapter 14 - How to Create the Perfect Pitch

How to earn funding for your projects and innovations.

Do not leave the scene of your first 90 days without a well-constructed pitch for investment, resources, or a sustainable transition project. In this chapter we go into how you leverage your induction period to design the pitch that gets the green light for change and transformation.

Chapter 15 - Better than average, not perfect

Is it good enough to be good enough?

I stuck this chapter in here because by now, you're thinking about how you're going to perfectly execute all my advice. Perfect execution is not the goal. The objective is to soak up the content and make some decisions about where you'd like to get started. I discuss some alternative ways to approach being better than average, but not perfect. Try it on, see how it feels.

At the risk of sounding like I'm pitching this at a pretty low bar, for most things you need to do at work, it's already exceptional to be better than average.

Read that again. It's already exceptional to be better than average.

Chapter 16 - Duds and Explosives

How to deal with a toxic boss or culture.

Like it says on the tin, this is the chapter with all the gunpowder. We are talking about the dark triad traits, gaslighting and what to do when you feel surrounded by rogues, or bosses who don't defend their teams. This chapter is very practical and resonant for many of us working in ultra-competitive environments, but still want to live by certain values and codes of conduct.

Chapter 17 - Support for your Journey

How to know if coaching or related services are right for you.

There are many ways we are challenged as leaders, and the number of ways is only set to grow as we approach planetary boundaries, cost of living crises and shortages everywhere. Here we discuss coaching, mentorship, and therapy as tools in your tool kit, as opposed to needs that you feel embarrassed about. Here's how to navigate your decision making on investing in one, all or none at all.

Epilogue - The Aligned Mission

Here we wrap up this book with the GRIPPS ™ concept, on how to take action and embed what you are called to do. We take a helicopter view of the book's main concepts, to help you choose a focus. Whilst this book is a high-level introduction to the concepts you will need, we go deeper on each aspect with workbooks and resources available on my website, and through my one to one and group programmes. The important thing is to walk away from reading this with a clear starting point in mind.

Other Good Stuff

In the final section of this book, I help you explore what's coming up next, and the wealth of resources and sources of inspiration that inspired me for this work. I hope you'll enjoy digging in!

Let's get started, shall we?

Context and the Case
for Change

Theme 1 –
The Planetary Dimension

"There are more stars in the universe than there is sand on every beach on earth"

**Carl Sagan, Author,
Astronomer, cosmologist**

As an armchair citizen-scientist with only entry level training in mathematics and sciences, I found this estimate to be mind-blowing and barely credible. As it turns out, mathematicians and astronomers appear to agree that this statement comparing stars to sand is likely true.

It's incredibly humbling to realise that the earth is hardly even a grain of sand in the context of the universe, yet it remains the only planet we've found that can potentially sustain the oxygen, water, food, and temperatures we need to survive and evolve; or looking at it another way, we evolved over billions of years for the precise conditions on our home planet.

Science matters. The debate around the genesis of life itself isn't likely to be definitively explained because the evidence likely no longer exists, but science and the scientific method gives us at least clues and methods of determining what's important to life, and how we can preserve it.

As the third planet from the sun, we've found reasonably stable conditions for the past 11.700 years or so. Prior to that, there were ice ages, mass extinction events, and a world made up of organisms that looked different to us. We've been living like goldilocks in the perfect zone, not too hot, nor too cold, dependable seasons, crops, water supplies. Yet our neighbouring planets of Mercury and Venus suffer runaway Greenhouse Gas effects.

Greenhouse Gases (GHGs) aren't inherently bad. Without them, the Earth's average temperature would be minus 18 degrees. The challenge we face today is that the level of all GHGs, and in particular CO_2 in the atmosphere, far exceeds any numbers estimated over the last 800,000 years of history. This is according to NOAA, the National Oceanic and Atmospheric Administration of the USA. GHGs act as a buffer and traps heat within our atmosphere. Too much of it too fast, and life on earth will become unbearable hot for most living species, without us having sufficient time to evolve naturally to these new temperatures.

Is the increase in CO2 a natural cyclical event? Many of the world's greatest scientific minds believe we are in the Anthropocene, a new epoch characterised by the significant impact humans and human activity now have on reshaping integrated systems on earth. By their estimations, humans have evolved to create exponential impact on their surroundings, enough to create our own mass extinction event.

This isn't about scare mongering. These are data and insight to inform our actions. I side with science. The new hallmark of a developed and mature society is one that can be sustained into the future indefinitely, so it makes sense that we would design economies that could survive and thrive. I fear though that we can just as easily go the way of other great societies in history and disappear, leaving only remnants of our former grandeur behind.

That we are thought to be in the Anthropocene isn't inherently good or bad - risk always walks in the hand of opportunity, and that's not just a saying in mandarin. For all the potentially negative effects of our actions, it is also possible to consider that we can reverse what we've done or do better going forward as we develop innovative technologies. Much of what we've learned about the way life works, we've learned in the last 200 years, and that knowledge stack is only being exponentially added to.

This is where opportunity is born dear reader.

If you are scientifically or statistically minded, there is no shortage of opportunity to add to the existing levels of knowledge, by exploring the technology and data at our disposal, to recreate, regenerate, redesign, adapt, and change in order to assure our survival on any problem you choose to address.

Three of the world's billionaires have used their considerable means to launch space missions. The intentions behind these missions vary from ego, to generating revenue through space tourism, to expanding the possibilities of science, to finding or creating new habitable zones for our species and others essential to our lives.

Although the idea of being a multi planet species is appealing and realistic in our lifetimes, the debate comes when we consider the opportunity cost of that focus, over solving problems right here and right now on earth, and the trade off this implies we could inadvertently be making, between saving lives without compromising any, or saving a few lives so that a species may survive in the very long term, possibly at the expense of many.

The ethical scale of what's at risk is often difficult to comprehend. We are capable of changing so much so quickly, it seems wise to slow down and consider carefully where we want to take our species, considering we don't know enough to make a perfectly informed choice.

Depending on who you listen to, we have anywhere between three years and 28 years before runaway systemic change becomes inevitable, and the earth will likely be unable to support human life. Whether you believe the forecasts or not, what's grounded in fact is that life is far more complex, and humans far more dependent on living ecosystems than the economic theories and models used to build our finance-based economies today.

As a basic example, both humans and plants are from the domain of life known as Eukarya. Plants evolved to use CO_2 as their building block and expel oxygen, where humans evolved to use oxygen for energy and expel CO_2. What phenomenal balance! It's a process we take for granted every day, yet when you study what's involved you realise your life is undoubtedly a miracle.

As another example, microbiologists estimate that our bodies are home to more than 100 million bacteria and harmless viruses, which either help our bodies to function, or do us no harm in most cases. All of our food is also teeming with them, and many are capable of surviving extreme temperatures. We owe our very existence to organisms we mischaracterised perhaps a little over 100 years ago as undesirable.

I want to close this topic of the environmental big picture on sustainability, by discussing the nine planetary boundaries, beyond which scientists recommend we should not go.

The understanding of the interconnected relationships of systems on earth has increased dramatically over the last 50 years, and now scientists are better able to describe how these relationships work and connect with each other, in such a way that we can have more control over how we positively influence them.

Johan Rockström, a Swedish scientist, led 28 other scientists in 2009 on the study of our planetary resilience. This work became the nine planetary boundaries used to frame the challenge before us, comprehensively, and backed by data. These boundaries implicate the macro understanding of our systems. The green zone represents the safe boundary. The yellow zone suggests increased risk of adverse consequences, and the red zone represents considerable risk to life and longevity.

The Nine Boundaries are:

Climate Change: The rate of global average change in temperature. The target is to keep temperatures under 1.5 degrees into the future. This means achieving stability between the CO_2 emitted and conversely extracted from the upper atmosphere. This is the most fundamental of the boundaries as it has implications for others. It is currently in the yellow zone.

Ocean Acidification: Oceans function as carbon sinks as marine organisms absorb carbon for their own use. High acidity reverses this process by destroying the shells and exoskeletal structures of marine life, leaving the organisms susceptible to death, further accelerating the process of CO_2 release and reduction in the efficacy of natural carbon sinks.

Stratospheric Ozone Depletion: The Ozone layer helps preserve our atmosphere, and filter ultraviolet rays. After a hole was discovered in the southern hemisphere in the 1980s, The Montreal protocol put in place controls over the release of gasses that were causing harm, eventually allowing for the recovery of much of the ozone layer. This is now safely in the green zone.

Biogeochemical flows: this refers to nitrogen and phosphorus mainly discharged from farms, that disrupt aquatic and marine ecosystems. Evidence of this exists in the Baltic Sea today with the phenomenon of Anoxia - a severe deficiency of oxygen has taken hold. This is considered to be in the red zone.

Rate of Biodiversity Loss: Wild ecosystems preserve necessary biodiversity that helps protect our life and climate. The fewer species we have, the higher the risk of population imbalances across the food chain, and the more potential exposure and susceptibility of humans to harm causing pathogens. Genetic diversity is considered to be in the red zone, while functional diversity is in the yellow zone.

Global Freshwater Use: Our demand and disruption of natural water systems affects both wildlife and human civilisation and is a source of significant geopolitical tension. As the earth warms, and glaciers melt, these tensions can become more significant, at risk to life. This has tipped into the yellow zone.

Land System Change: Today, monoculture crop land is a net source of greenhouse gases, where forests are a net carbon sink. Reversing this trend requires a review of farming methods and consumption practices such that more regenerative and natural strategies are employed.

Aerosol Loading: Aerosols which are suspensions of solid particles or liquid in the air that we breathe, impact our life expectancy. They also disrupt rain and cooling patterns in the upper atmosphere. Too high loading also damages the ozone layer. This is now in the yellow zone.

Chemical Pollution/ Novel entities: Radioactive compounds and heavy metals impact ecosystems and life expectancy in water, soil, and the air, and can be the source of new potentially damaging combinations and consequences. There are 10s of thousands of man-made chemical compounds considered under this heading, and there's not a lot of knowledge of what the consequences can be of the accumulation of these over time. We do not currently have a measure of what is an appropriate level.

These 9 boundaries are listed here under a creative commons license, referenced at the end of this book.

The challenge before us is to improve those boundaries lying in the danger zones and maintain or improve other boundaries. Is this something your work and training can help you contribute to preserving?

We don't all need to be scientists, but it's helpful if we understand that we need scientific insight in our decision making, because to base our actions on financial metrics only is fraught with significant long-term business risk if we depend on the earth's resources for those outcomes we seek.

Theme 2 –
The Socio - Economic Dimension

Many of us grew up in an education system that taught us how to maximise wealth, and that our individual achievements actually held premium value within our local communities and wider society.

In my case, this gave me a heightened sense of my own ego and pride from an early age, as well as a fiery drive and determination to excel at my chosen disciplines. It also gave me an absolute fear of undertaking things that I didn't immediately prove to be good at. Both these dimensions had long term consequences on my decision making into adulthood.

If you've also had this conditioning, you likely still have it today. It may or may not play out in the job you're doing right now. More than likely, it impacts the way you raise your kids. It's a compelling narrative, right? Being better than everyone around you tends to be a strong part of how we define our successes.

The challenge I'm going to present you with today, is that there are other narratives that serve some of the same end games you have in mind. What if, instead of maximising wealth you sub optimised wealth in exchange for maximising your positive impact? Would you feel as good? Maximising impact as a business owner, would mean that you are able to comprehensively satisfy your needs, your shareholders, employees, customers, suppliers, and the community you are a part of. In many ways it is harder to do than profit maximisation; can the challenge in itself be more rewarding in the end?

When I was 24, I became a *Big Sister*. It was an international outreach programme, where we partnered with an orphaned child, to help support them in their growth, social and professional development. She came from a family of eight children. Her mother was killed, and her father imprisoned. Two of her sisters had also been at the orphan home. She wasn't sure where her other siblings were.

She found it difficult to open up to me; much of what I learned about her came from the home. Her understanding of relationships with adults was to ask for and receive gifts, outfits, a box of Kentucky Fried Chicken, jewellery, hairdressing appointments. Everything else was off limits, things she would not discuss. Naïve as I was, it wasn't what I had expected when I signed up, and after six months, I quit the programme. I wasn't ready to come face to face with so much hardship, psychological trauma, and didn't know how to be the big sister she needed without being the big sister she wanted. I failed at being a big sister.

The experience remained with me. Two years after this, I began travelling the world, and appreciating different sides to the socio-economic issues that abound in what is now called the global south (though I can't say I like the term). I saw children working on farms with their parents, or selling on the streets, between traffic lights. I saw children and families living under really challenging circumstances, limited pipe borne potable water, horrendous sanitation conditions. I saw kids and adults starving. I also saw many with barely enough to survive, who were happy, playing, creating little moments of fun without the trappings of tablets, or video games.

Money doesn't seem to translate into happiness, but our individual or communal relationships with having or not having it, as well as the physical conditions of where we live, actually seemed to make the most difference to whether someone was content enough in their circumstances, or miserable.

When I travelled to Uganda, Cambodia, Uzbekistan, and Honduras to name a few, I met people I thought would be desperate about their circumstances, behaving joyfully. The people who seemed the least kind, and considerate, were the wealthy folk in big cities of major economies. I'm not sure how "more" got to become the goal, rather than happiness and enjoying what you have.

I was hardly different from any of the unhappy wealthy folk I describe above. With a passion for big cities and bigger careers, the more I earned the more I wanted to earn. There wasn't space to doubt myself and my intentions ever, I was too busy in the doing and achieving. I judged people like my little sister from the programme, and others that I met on my travels, as lacking ambition, or being too under educated to understand what they were clearly missing. Today I know I was in many ways the ignorant one.

The Cuckoo in the nest of the last 50 years, has been the successful efforts at treating and teaching economics as a scientific discipline. Milton Friedman is often discussed as the father of shareholder capitalism. In 1970 he wrote his pièce de résistance, advocating that the role of business is to maximise profits. You can read this article from the archives of the New York Times, titled the Friedman doctrine.

In that article Friedman mentions conforming to social rules, and customs as the limit to shareholder primacy. When an organisation crosses borders for trade, whose rules, and customs should abide? And can and should an organisation act differently depending on where they are located? The ethical questions here are immense, yet for most of the last 50 years organisations have simply chosen the path most profitable, without considering the ethics.

It was suggested that corporations don't have responsibilities except to the law that created them, while individuals carry different responsibilities in their personal lives, which they can address as shareholders upon receipt of dividends. I believe this thinking is flawed, not least because laws lag well behind our collective and systemic understanding of phenomenon in our world.

What this article and much of the economic literature of that time and today does not consider enough, is integrated systems thinking. Some thinkers argue that even when shareholders act in the interest of profit maximisation, they are more likely to design better social relevant and climate considered solutions if they are appropriately incentivised to do so (with taxes and subsidies). The challenge is that the taxes and subsidies lag behind typically due to lobbying activity.

Economics is a bit of "dirty" science. I use this term in reference to an economic term called a "dirty floating exchange rate" where the exchange rates are manipulated by control over demand and supply to keep them stable. This same phenomenon happens when political aspirations and policy meet. The radical changes needed often don't happen, because there's a lot of trade-offs and compromises to keep the balance. The models are thus flawed because they do not consider corruption, special interests, and other economic activity not formally recognised in the model. Economic models appear to veer far from what happens in the real world, but there is a notable exception, *The Doughnut Economics Model* introduced by Kate Raworth, and as derived by the doughnut economics org.

In brief, *Doughnut Economics* sets two bands: a social foundation beneath which no one should slip and an outer-band or ecological ceiling beyond which we should not exceed. Inside the doughnut, is the safe and just space for humanity where we are thought to be happiest. Beyond the doughnut's ring, only darkness comes.

As business leaders, a just goal for our shared near future is to find ways to bring this substance filled ring of doughnut to life, without tipping off the edges on either side. We will discuss the many ways we can deliver this.

Traditional corporate social responsibility and philanthropy are inadequate for our times. Leaders must rethink what a business is and how it drives changes in the world.
    "Net Positive" by Paul Polman and Andrew S. Winston.

I want to introduce the concept of Net-positive, as it's a central tenet of this book. We have heard so much in the last UN conference of the parties (COP26) about net-zero goals and targets, but in my view, we're beyond all that now - Net Zero in 2050 means very little if the biggest actors and contributors to climate change and ecological disaster cannot be Net-positive by 2030.

Net-positive is being able to say yes to the question: is your business or career contributing positively to the world, more than it takes away? In their book of the same name, Andrew Winston, and Paul Polman, talk at length about Paul's role in Unilever to alter the company's carbon and social footprint. Microsoft as an economic powerhouse and social actor are also discussed in the book, particularly around their commitment to be *Net-positive* by 2030 and to have removed all the CO_2 they ever added to the earth's atmosphere since they were created in 1975 by 2050. That's a big hairy goal if I ever heard one.

Yet *Net-positive* isn't just about carbon. It's about looking beyond profit to extract more from what we do every day in a way that appeals to all our stakeholders. We need to start rewriting our narratives from the words, philosophies, and actions of men like Milton Friedman and Jack Welch who championed the shareholder capitalism revolution of the 70s and 80s.

How we live within a system matters. No matter who you are, you are dependent, and you influence the system, so let's figure out how best to plot your career as needed to create the momentum shifts with what you do for work, and in how you contribute.

Theme 3 - Governing the System

A perfect market doesn't exist. Economists and pro-capitalists argue that the market will decide what it values most, but this assumption fails because of any or all of the following real situations that occur daily.

- **We do not assign a value to nature**. Even if we did, we don't have perfect information about how that value should be attributed. Furthermore, as we learn more, information asymmetry means that knowledge isn't evenly distributed.

- **We are not rational beings**. This may be the most flawed of all assumptions in economic theory. As humans we are complex psychologically. Our actions often come from many layers of thought; for example, short term vs long term, satisfying physical needs vs psychological needs, acting in the interest of self, family, or an even broader lens, or based on culture, systems, and beliefs. The way we make decisions is complex, so it's actually illogical to assume we will act logically - pardon the irony.

- **Corruption, a kin friend to marketing.** I am only half kidding with this one. There are many who seek to influence others with false information. This could represent itself in the form of marketing promotions, public relations, debates, editorials, social media. Once it's possible to corrupt a system without consequence, a perfect market cannot exist. Marketing with an inclusive agenda and big picture intentions behind it isn't inherently bad. It only tips into a negative light when linked to the topic below.

- **Ego and Self Interest tends to trump altruism.** Legacy creation is a feature of our human condition. That desire to be remembered and create something that lasts can be beneficial but cannot be relied upon to deliver benefits to all society. Deep altruism is rare, perhaps as a consequence of cultures, survivalism, beliefs, mental training, and past experiences of breaches of trust. Ego and excessive self-interest can be overcome by more altruism and empathy. One of the interesting personalities to learn about and study when exploring altruism is the Frenchman Matthieu Ricard, holder of a PHD in Molecular genetics, turned author and Buddhist monk. He participated in a study on the effects of meditation on the brain, and on the occurrence of altruism. In that study, it is clear that meditation can increase neuroplasticity, enhance connections, and change the size of distinct parts of your brain, just after a few weeks of that practice, regardless of age. This opens the door to the idea that kindness and compassion can be skills we can develop through training.

- **Ethical questions.** The current technological revolution – the 4th industrial revolution as it is billed, is bringing into sharp review the vast number of ethical questions we are now faced with as a global society, because of the volume data, processing capacity, and new net knowledge that we are accumulating, albeit in an imbalanced distribution. Ethical questions include:

    a) the rights of all living things, and not just humans to exist and thrive on earth.

    b) The rights of artificially intelligent machines to exist, and to potentially have self-determination in the future.

    c) The right to health care, which can one day include treatments that could extend human life well beyond 100 years.

    d) Ownership rights for land, and resources in space.

    e) Justice for climate change, biodiversity loss, pollution, and waste.

    f) The right of humans and other living organisms to equity and inclusion.

    g) The right to privacy.

    h) The right to terminate one's own life.

    i) The right to fairness and justice in our legal and economic systems.

The list is in no way exhaustive. The level of change we are about to experience whether or not we take action on climate change is immense, and as a practitioner of change for many years, it is without doubt that we need strong systems of governance in place, not to decide on the answers, but to facilitate that the answers are decided based on collective and equitable input.

I don't believe free markets can do this, or one single ideology, religion, or discipline of science either. It feels more like we need an ark; with equal and distributed representation, and tower of babel types as interpreters, so that we can weigh the interest of all parties.

We have a history of cooperation, not just with other humans, but with the living world as evidenced in our biochemistry. How can we design the next paradigm of governance, which addresses the inefficiencies of the systems of economics, politics, and social reforms that have not served our interest in the past?

This sounds like yet another great intellectual challenge, that **your** skills may well be suited for.

Part 1:

Your Environment and You

Your pathway to self-mastery

CHAPTER 1

If it's important, build a model

Creating a conscious self-improvement plan

M ental models are the way we navigate the world around us, a system through which we make choices and decisions, whether consciously or not. We are perhaps more aware of them when we learn from procedures and practices at work. They may resemble continuous improvement tools, decision making frameworks, quality standards, sequential activities, or project and change management methodologies. They are also present in the unstructured decision making that we do, somewhat insidiously and unconsciously.

Mental models help us make rapid decisions in contexts where we are bombarded with decisions and mental stimulation for prolonged periods. They help us break complex decisions down into simpler decision-making frameworks and routines, and eventually they also become habitual, autonomous, and routine for us as we execute our day-to-day functions.

The keys to mental models and their relationship with behaviours is to first understand them, identify them, and have a general sense for when they apply, and when other frameworks may be needed. To make meaningful changes in your life or in the business around you, you need to tap into your strengths, by identifying the mental models that make those strengths meaningful to you.

There are two authorities on the topic of mental models and habits that I've found interesting and stimulating to reference and learn from. I will reference them both in the resource sheet at the end of this book. But for now, spare a moment to think about all the models you've come across that have been useful for decisions you make at work and at home. You probably have a Top 10: see if you can list them.

Some commonly used if not consciously evaluated mental models.

The 80/20 Rule - according to Pareto states that 80% of the output comes from 20% of the input, in simple terms. Applying this to work, the rule suggests that there are a few activities or inputs that are critical to the outcome you expect in any circumstance, if you were to find and focus on those, you'd make a greater impact while spending less time and effort. I don't know about you, but I can easily see how pareto can apply to my daily to do list, my goals list, the places I want to visit, the things I want to buy, the people I want to spend time with. Most of what we do, doesn't matter, the key is to know the 20% that does.

Root Cause Analysis - If you've worked in Finance, Supply chain, Quality, Engineering, project management and IT, perhaps much of your working life has been dominated by models for root cause analysis.

These come in two forms. There are statistical models driven by data points. Your organisation may be set up to capture multiple data points along a product journey, to evaluate statistical variations from a predetermined mean. Or you may have used tools specific to investigative and qualitative reviews, such as 6W2H - and 5 Whys - (6W2H - What, Where, When, Why, Who, Whom, How and How Much).

Either way, these techniques help you to dig deeper into past failures and determine future possible failures using what is called failure mode and effect analysis.

This is all jargony mumbo jumbo if you haven't had this experience and that's okay because all they mean is this: We can apply methods to diagnose or anticipate failures, then learn from them. Applied to normal life, have you ever reflected on why something you did actually helped, or hurt you in the past? That's what root cause analysis does.

Have you ever used that knowledge to control something for the future? You get the idea. You already do this; the question is to what extent you apply it across the critical paths for your life.

The final global model I'd like to explore is Systems Theory - This is a philosophy that looks at complexity not through the sum of its parts, but by examining the relationships among other things in that system. This can apply to man-made systems, and to ecosystems or biological systems. It is about how things interrelate with each other that matter most when seeking change, so that the complete system continues to function as required, or to make improvements.

I gave earlier an example of this with the microbiome that lives within us serving useful functions such as break down of essential minerals for our bodies or protection against disease, while they derive what they need to live from the conditions created by our bodies. But systems aren't always positive. Sometimes you want to break the chains of a system.

A historic example would be systems of slavery and oppression. Much has been done to change this system, and laws written in support of it, but unfortunately, we can still find examples of slavery and human rights abuses today.

I've chosen these three to explain, as they perhaps carry a great weight for the journey we are on together in these pages. From the perspective of finding your purpose, perhaps what you seek; happiness, wealth, health, freedom, can be sourced by focusing on very few things that will make the lever shift in the direction you want to travel.

There is a related model in economics called the concentration ratio, which I find helpful to explain. The concentration ratio is used in economics and statistics to illustrate the relative sizes of firms compared to the industry that they are in. It is estimated that the top three to five firms in many major industries today typically control 60-80% of the market, or the resources in a given geography or domain. Applying this to ourselves, there are probably three to five thought patterns that are currently dictating everything you do. How can you master these and bend your own mind to your will?

I'm sure you can find creative ways to look at your life using established models, but what of your own? I like to say that your success has secrets that only you know. It's entirely about how you leverage your knowledge, talent, skill, courage, and resilience, with your own systems and models to scale or repeat positive outcomes, even when the rules of the game are changing. That's worth tapping into wouldn't you say? We will go into this topic in more detail in Chapter 2.

Mental models can also form cognitive biases.

Other common models can be benign and often under-recognised but can eventually form part of your neural network of biases, informing your decision making. Bias is a feature not a bug. It's our brains' way of making us more responsive in decision making particularly when our immediate safety is concerned and evolved at a time when we faced numerous short-term threats to life and livelihood.

In *Thinking fast and slow* by Daniel Kahneman, he discusses decision making heuristics, and describes some of our biases as playing into our fast-thinking modes. Slow thinking is something we train to improve at, particularly when the concerns to life and livelihood are now understood to be integrated, interconnected, and complex.

Start with understanding your own biases. What are the biases you're using to make decisions? How can you employ a healthy curiosity to find out if your assumptions are valid or invalid from time to time? Biases become problematic when they are illegal, harmful, and unacknowledged.

Bias is usually also coupled with privilege, both for those who have privilege, and those who crave it. We've been socialised in popular culture to believe that those who have more and earn more, must be more, and this permeates all our interactions.

Ever reacted emotionally to a trigger? This is also a feature of bias; previous experiences inform us that when a particular sequence of events happens, it must mean that the sequence will be completed in the same way we experienced some trauma in the past. It's not that we are actually being hurt or attacked, it just feels like that because that trigger has hacked into our sensory perceptions.

Let's explore some other ways bias appears in our everyday interactions.

- **Confirmation bias** - our brains tend to seek out evidence that confirms its existing perceptions and theories.

- **Affinity bias** - we seek out others with similar values to form affinity groups.

- **Attribution bias** - we interpret the actions of others from our own viewpoints then make decisions based on what we have attributed to them.

- **Anchoring bias** - when you are overly focussed on the first piece of information provided. (Often used as a tactic in negotiations, for example salaries)

- **Bandwagon effect** - a classic form of *groupthink*, where others adopting an opinion publicly will make it more likely that more people will adopt the same opinion.

- **Clustering illusion** - the tendency to see patterns where the events are actually random.

Finally, there's the **Blind spot bias** - which is the point of discussing this; many of us fail to recognise our own biases in the way that we do others. And this is where self-mastery comes in, it's not about being perfect; it's about seeing yourself as you are, without the illusory effects, and about acceptance, and where feasible, growth.

We break bias by embracing it as a tool. We are more likely to consider our biases and how to evolve them, if we understand that they are coping mechanisms for us to operate, instead of rules. Our biases are heavily linked to our mental models and understanding this clears the path to improvement.

Developing your Personal Models

If you have a sense of accomplishment about anything in your life, go back to that thing and examine how you did that. For most of us our models are fine blends of popular culture, training, practice, and skill, trial, and error. Whatever the source, unlock those secrets, and explore how repeatable they are. Here's an example from a friend of mine, on *Where Ideas Launch – the sustainable innovation podcast.*

"I consider my life so far based on my professional experience as a little bit of a computer game. When you go from one level to the other, you collect achievements and then unlock some next level and you get to fight the boss demons. So that's exactly what my journey has been so far. As I grew in my career in social impact, I knew I'd need very special tools and weapons and experience and knowledge to fight that battle for change. And once I worked with NGOs for a while, I understood that there was always a need to chase the money, as it's so hard to actually get enough funds to do all the good that needs to be done. So, I became curious about where the money comes from, and how to redirect it toward the purpose I imagined."

Quote from Anna Derinova-Hartmann – On Where Ideas Launch – Sustainable Innovation Podcast episode 10 – Leverage your Strengths for Social Good

I loved Anna's analogy. It's a gamified way to think about the skills and experiences you are building, toward an overall goal, as you construct meaning from your career. Anna has coded things into levels to give meaning to her thought process, and it also helps her to use storytelling to share her journey and approach. We will work more on unearthing your model in Chapter 2.

A personal model gives you a repeatable tested framework for navigating decisions. Without them, tasks as simple as getting dressed in the morning, to as complicated as building a medical instrument become exponentially harder, if you are redesigning every time. Models help us reduce decision making friction from our lives, so we can have more peace. They mould our habits and help them fit within a higher purpose for our existence.

CHAPTER 2

Who are you, really?

How to begin a self-discovery journey

Who are you really?

I n all the work I do, I'm constantly awake to the genius of the people around me. It's something that I believe to be unique to everyone, and most people and even organisations have a tough time finding theirs, so I thought I'd help out.

No one can define your lane but you. If you're familiar with the term blue ocean strategy around how we explore unfamiliar territory as a pioneer, instead of competing for the spoils in the red ocean with the masses, finding your own lane is a blue ocean

57

for your next opportunity in this rapidly evolving landscape of our planet, and beyond it.

When you are effectively navigating and sensing your way through new terrain, you begin to accumulate insight that helps with each successive step.

I use the word sensing because words matter. If we spend our life "looking" for things, we may miss out on all that we can hear, taste, touch, feel and otherwise perceive and intuitively sense. Vision is too narrow a definition for what makes up our human consciousness.

Katherine Ann Byam

I want to talk about the lovely big eared elephant in the room.

Every day there's a new solution, digital application or artificial intelligence algorithm that optimises another operational task that you are extraordinarily skilled at. Your gift to the world, therefore, isn't only in what you can do operationally, although this is a part of it. It's also not about what you know because knowledge is growing increasingly ubiquitous. Your gift, my friend, is about what you can create, connect, change, and influence, using the unique combination of all of those influences on the way you think, strategize, and do.

More resources today are being allocated to those who can generate influence on the world around them, either through their exceptional thought leadership and scientific rigour in solving global challenges, or by their ability to sway others to some desirable way of thinking; regardless perhaps of who desires it.

It therefore stands to reason that if your job isn't more than 50% about innovation or creativity, consider that its obsolescence is inevitable. One way to deal with that reality is to actively make your job obsolete as it will certainly stir up creativity. A green revolution is underway, while other factions of society want to maintain the status quo. There are opportunities on both sides of the thought divide and in the space in the middle, the question only remains whether you want to take the long view, or the short view.

Perhaps these words are stirring some anxiety for you. People often say to me: *I'm not that creative, I'm not sure I can do that, or perhaps I'm comfortable as I am.* I want to make this clear to you right now. Comfort is a choice. It's as valid a choice as growth, regression, or quitting all together. I only ask that you make the choice, and not let your choice be clouded by the judgement of others.

Perhaps you don't remember it, but we all started curiously, and found innovative ways to do things our parents either didn't like, laughed at, or grew hyper and nervous about. When we're younger, people think our quirks and unique personality traits are cute and funny. As we start maturing, the fitting in expectation grows stronger.

Thankfully in some areas, there is a momentum shift to embracing our differences and being inclusive in how we lead. The question is, how do we reverse years of trying to fit in, and suddenly become who we are?

The answer is we don't, not suddenly anyway, rediscovering yourself is a bit like going through puberty again. You are going to have to try things on, see what fits, and give things a chance. Part of that process can be taking a trip back to some of those early years when you were freer. You've probably developed skills, affinities and acute awareness of some things that have become really important to you, and serve as hobbies, or interests, you just never considered them because you weren't sure how to monetise them. Or perhaps time, experiences, travel, work have exposed you to entirely new areas that you'd maybe fancy having a play with.

It's time to awaken what's lying dormant within you. It is a fact to say that we cannot completely navigate the world without considering our impact on others, as in the long run there will be costs to that exclusion. Yet I'd argue the greatest cost you'll ever bear is to yourself and the denial of your own purpose. You'll know how well you're doing on your self-discovery journey by how much you can reduce the friction among these four things, without losing your unique energy in the process:

- Managing the expectations of family and friends.
- Managing organisational feedback designed for efficiency and not creativity.
- Managing customer feedback.

- Navigating the society, you live in so that swimming in your lane can happen within the risk and safety appetite you have chosen for your life.

Life is a Venn diagram. It's 100% about intersectionality, of ideas, skills, capacity, resources, conditions, desires, basic needs. Risks, opportunities, others.

Without emotional intelligence to manage these trade-offs and the ability to optimise some things and sub-optimise others, you're not going to be good at doing any business. Keep in mind however that being good in business does not always coincide with being good at life, but it's possible to be. In the long-term scheme of things, what's good for you, is good for the planet, if we are assuming that you want long life, health, and happiness.

If these desires are not of your heart that's perfectly valid also. Be aware though, that you may meet some significant opposition if you choose to the short-term wealth maximisation route.

Being authentically you is important. It's also essential to understand that any right you claim for yourself, others will claim too. To survive and thrive in a world where we all are different, it requires the four Rs of Respect, Recognition, Reassurance and Responsibility.

Swimming in your own lane, or finding your genius, is about first spending the time to go deep within, before stepping out again and crafting a strategy to navigate the world as yourself, PROUD, yet textured by the nuances of the society and communities you live in.

Katherine Ann Byam

Here are a few tips to approach finding your lane.

- Start with Why. Do you have a clearly elaborated "why" statement for your choice of career or job that you revisit from time to time? How has it evolved and changed in the last six months for you?

- What are your skills, strengths, and weaknesses? Also consider your passion, and that which gives you energy. How can these be leveraged to address your why?

- Explore the context. What's changing in the world, and how do those changes create opportunities for you, and or risks?

- What problems need solving related to your why, your skills and your context, and what's there to explore either locally to you, or on a bigger scale?

- Pax animi - peace of mind. What would bring peace of mind to your customer, employer, or relevant interest group? Have you considered what good looks like?

- What's the short- and long-term perspective of these ideas that are coming up for you, and how can you take exploratory action?

- If not here, where? Would it be useful for you to completely change your context?

- Is the timing right for your idea?

- Who is in your camp? Who can help you realise your idea?

- Who is the recipient of this new reality you are creating, and what are their thoughts on it?

One of my favourite random interactions of the last three years, was meeting Shane Ward, a guest on both of my podcasts, a filmmaker turned Agro-ecologist. I spoke to him off air at the end of the episode 29 of Where Ideas Launch – The Sustainable Innovation Podcast called *Feeding the World* and realised that many times the path to arriving at where you need to be, isn't a straight line, but instead a beautiful mosaic.

Here's a longish quote from the second interview I set up with him on *Do What Matters - Career & Leadership on Purpose Podcast*. I've had to edit bits to bring a shorter quote to you in the book, but the entire episode is a great listen.

"I suppose the thing about a life is that it doesn't tend to neatly follow chapter markers. I started my first career in Australia out of high school moving in to film and television – as I really wanted to be a film director – but didn't have any idea about how to do that. I tried going to university, doing an Arts degree (in philosophy, art history and cinema studies) but that didn't pan out and I ended up working low paid jobs before eventually finding my way to film school. I was very driven, determined and laser focussed on that one thing, that career choice. Then I had a period of crisis in my life precipitated by a death, a breakup, an injury, and things kind of fell apart. I decided to rebuild my life as I wanted it to be, and left Australia for Europe. Soon after finding myself in Cannes at Hollywood parties and pitching my projects to film executives.

That journey brought me later to London where I inadvertently fell into the corporate world, where my skills as an independent filmmaker (writing scripts, building websites, designing graphics, directing actors, managing teams, budgets and schedules) and constant creative problem solving stood me in good stead. Before long I became a communications manager, and then after a succession of roles for several FTSE100 companies had carved out something of a niche for myself as a strategy and digital comms specialist. I had reached this level by learning and *adapting as I went, harnessing and developing my skills and an attitude of "can do". I continued to do film projects on the side, never abandoning my film career, but at the point where I was in my early 30's I may have been earning pretty decent money, but I had to admit that I was deeply unsatisfied and my mental health was not in a great place.*

I needed another break to find my compass bearing, and so I set of on another adventure. It was while learning to scuba dive around the coral reefs and cenotés of Mexico's Yucatan peninsula that I came across an unexpected opportunity, and after meeting up with my girlfriend in Belize and then travelling to Brazil that we decided (quite on a whim) to buy a house in Mexico. Our plan was to work the rest of the year in London, quit our jobs and move there – so we did exactly that. It turned out to be quite a pivotal moment for me because it was living there, surrounded by jungle and sea that I realised how important my connection to the natural world was. Up until that point I had been caught up in the big city life, and although I had enjoyed the energy of it, I realised it was also draining me. I can still remember the moment in Mexico, standing outside of my house looking at the wind blowing through the jungle, the sound of it in the trees, and I suddenly felt energised, alive. This was the first domino to fall for me, a connection made that would pave the way for what was to come."

Shane went on to learn permaculture, agroforestry and even returned to study at university (completing a degree in ecology) before founding his own ecological consultancy Action Ecology that provides regenerative land use design and advisory services now based in Auckland New Zealand. His communication and film making skills are still put to good use also, though now in support of his business and wider education with a focus on regenerative agriculture and sustainability.

He believes that there are three key themes that he developed throughout his life experiences that are the key ingredients to any career, they are:

- Systems thinking
- Storytelling
- Problem solving

Having the perception of things as interconnected and valuing those connections has threaded through all of his career pivots. The ability to communicate, and the constant development of how to do that better and reach people where they are, has also linked his career decisions together. The ability to accept the reality of a situation and pragmatically find ways to solve problems has helped him deliver consistently on the other two skills.

The more you can develop these three skills, the more adaptable you become at pivoting and changing, and the more capable at influencing others.

Bringing Shane's story to life was an honour for me, and it came about only because I had the courage to ask a stranger to talk to me. Remember that every new possibility that ever came to life started with a question. You can listen to the complete episode 2 of the podcast Do What Matters – Career and Leadership on Purpose Podcast for our full interview.

Mind-Map your way to success.

I love the work of the late Tony Buzan who developed mind mapping as a technique to mirror the way the brain works to activate more of its potential. It's a terrific way to get clarity on how your mind naturally processes something and leaves you with a structure you will completely understand.

Before you undertake this exercise or utilise the booklet in the link provided at the end of this book, I recommend you create the environment first. Artefacts and symbols matter. Every time you prepare for a reflective exercise, I recommend following the same preparation routines so that the routines and the artefacts trigger your body and then your mind to get into a welcoming state.

The standard kit you need for personal self-mastery work is as follows:

- A 5-subject notebook (or a Microsoft One Note Template with 5 Tabs, or a Remarkable or similar type notebook)

- A pen and highlighters in three distinct colours (or a stylus)

- A space that gives you an excess feeling of psychological safety. For me it's a cafe. A *Pain Quotidien* that's off the main street in London has always been my go-to place, but perhaps this exists or can be created in your home.

- The important thing is to transform that space either with artefacts, music, or lighting into your creative zone so that you can repeat the energy and vibe of your past creations there, whenever you re-visit it.

❖ Mind Mapping Exercise

There's no fixed structure for a mind map, but to get you started, draw the outline of a brain, human head, or face - or any way you deem appropriate to represent your brain.

Outline one by one some random sections, at roughly the same size, and start jotting what comes to mind.

Here are some thinking prompts to use for this work: ask what and why for all of these, and jot your answers

- My childhood pleasures
- My early successes
- What my family thinks I'm good at
- What I think I'm good at.
- You at your absolute best
- My greatest lessons
- My favourite job
- My favourite hobby
- What I'm most grateful for
- Any other relevant prompts that stir a story in you.

Extract from all these themes the bits that resonate with you and seem to fit with the person you are working on becoming.

Capture Flow

Turn the page on your mind map, and now it's time for your notebook. Here's a quote to get us started on Flow.

"The best moments in our lives are not the passive, receptive, relaxing times . . . The best moments usually occur if a person's body or mind is stretched to its limits in a voluntary effort to accomplish something difficult and worthwhile"

(Csikszentmihalyi, 1990)

I read the book Flow in the late 2000s; it helped me put into words experiences I already knew I had. By way of explanation, I'll outline my most vivid personal memory of flow, which will support the explanation of the concept.

As a plus sized teenager, most people didn't expect much from me in the way of sporting prowess, but my brothers knew me well and knew what I was capable of, so they pushed me to enter the school sports day table tennis championship. I was 13 years old at the time, and fully subscribed then to the effects of body dysmorphia on confidence and ability.

Most of the school didn't know I was the national under ten champion four years before this, because I stopped playing competitively, perhaps because I didn't want to fail, as I alluded to in an earlier chapter.

My brothers convinced me to compete not just in my age group, but against any girl at the college. The semi-final match took place in the school auditorium. I beat someone three years older than me and one of the most popular girls in the school, as she was objectively speaking, beautiful, and there was a great deal of expectation on her. She was so embarrassed she didn't finish the match, she walked away with a stream of tears running down her face.

In the final match, I had a big audience. I faced someone my own age, the sportiest, strongest, and fittest girl in my school year. She was a cadet, footballer, and a runner. EVERYONE expected her to win. Except I would not lose.

I don't remember the whole sequence of events. The score at the end was two sets to 1 in my favour. What I do remember is that I had a weakness that everyone knew about. My backhand. She was determined to exploit it and I was determined not to let it break.

In my memory, my peripheral vision was cloudy grey. I knew my brothers and many others from my class were watching, but I wasn't paying them any attention. My focus was completely on following the ball, and my opponent. Follow the ball, mark my competitor, position the racket, make her play the next shot.

When I got the opportunity of a forehand to strike, I'd take it without a moment's hesitation. I also had the sporting advantage of being left-handed, which means an unexpected strike power coming from that wing for most people not used to playing lefties. The *Rafael Nadal effect*. I used my strengths sparingly and decisively and hyper focussed on my weaknesses into a worthwhile defence. I remember the expression of pride on the faces of my brothers. How did she turn around her backhand like that?

My opponent wasn't pleased, but she accepted her defeat. To this day, I think that match is responsible for the great relationship we still have. She went on to be a football coach and fitness instructor. I never played another seriously competitive match of table tennis. But what I took away, is that I'm capable of engineering my game (aka, strategies, mental models, tactics) to rise to my best on will.

In your moments of flow, you truly understand what you're capable of, and It's typically more than you imagined. Spend some time to capture those moments and harvest them for the future you're creating.

71

The cast in your movie

This isn't a vanity question, although I'm drawn to ask who do you think should play you in a movie? I'm going with Lizzo and one of her big girrrls perhaps, because she's feisty, determined, sings well, and represents for her group perfectly. There's a lot you can learn about yourself by the characters you'd cast in your movie.

Spend some time to outline, while looking backward at your life, who's character and opinions most shaped your own views. Consider three people, and they can include a family member, friend, or teacher, sporting, or television personality, or even a fictitious character. Consider what they did for you then, and how that impacts you today.

To bring it all together, review your mind map and notes and highlight recurring themes, and the elements that speak loudest to you, that are worthy of further exploration. Use it to determine what you're curious about, what brings you joy, gives you hope, restores your energy, and or awakens your passion. Use what comes up as the baseline for your transition plan.

CHAPTER 3

Career Models

Types of career paths to deliver on your purpose

Why do you need a job and what purpose does it fulfil in your life?

I am going to introduce you to nine career profiles. Most of us have never had these nine options presented to us before we have to pick a course of study or career, or method for earning enough to enable the life we want to lead.

Before we get into the nine types of careers however, I think it's worthwhile discussing how we value our time and attention, arguably the most precious commodities we have sole dominion over.

I believe that time, attention, and purpose all have a deeply intertwined relationship.

There are billion-dollar industries being raised, funded, and scaled every day to either:

- Keep the attention of our time so that our attention can be monetised.

- Optimise the use of our time by making things quicker and more effective.

- Acquire our time, trading it off for monetary, social, or crypto rewards.

Consider the following when contemplating what's next for you and your time.

The Monetary valuation: Basic salary plus bonuses, car, pension, dental, healthcare, and other benefits. Personal pension contributions from your employer, benefits in kind that you receive – all of this net of taxes, then divide it by your hours of work – the REAL hours you work, not what your contract says.

Opportunity Cost valuation: If you were not spending your time in your current vocation/ or activity, what other vocations could you pursue, and how much could you earn in monetary, social, or crypto currency?

Purpose valuation: What if you could measure value in units of social or environmental impact? We currently have measures for CO_2 and other gases, but we also need scores for biodiversity on land and sea, water, and land pollution levels, etc.

Information isn't perfect, even in monetary terms. Although there is a growing movement for basic salaries to be made publicly available on every job, it's far from being the norm. It gets increasingly more difficult to assign a comparable value, in a common unit of measure for opportunity costs and impact, but perhaps if you can get to an equivalent opportunity cost or lower, and an impact that can be considered net positive, you have a match?

How you value your time, is how you value your purpose. With the above understanding, I now introduce you to these nine career profiles, which can support your long-term goal fulfilment. It's key to note that your *Ikigai* zone, can come from more than one of these approaches simultaneously. The purpose of this chapter is to plant the seed of open thinking in all of my readers, because perhaps there are opportunities you've overlooked.

❖ *Career Profile 1 - Gig to Great*

Here's someone who is not necessarily committed to the job that they have per se, but to the lifestyle or simplicity they want usually during a specific period of time. Typically, this is someone travelling the world and looking for gigs to pay the bills, or someone working an extra job to raise funds for some cause in their life. The job isn't the important thing, it's more about the life that you're able to have, the opportunity you unlock or the pain you avoid.

This is seldom the type of job where you'd work overtime, you pretty much do the gig and leave. There are some people who do this in an official job as opposed to a gig and I call this the sleepy hollow, as I think either the employer or the individual, haven't woken up to the potential they're missing out on by just getting by with the bare minimum. It can be pretty soul destroying if you do such a job year after year until retirement unless you've cleverly employed yourself with one or more of the other career profiles.

❖ Career Profile 2 - The Impact Maker

This is a bit of a misnomer because all jobs create impact, the question is whether it's positive or negative. For the purpose of the definition let's consider we are talking about *net-positive* impact.

This persona is like your Greta Thunberg. An activist, outspoken and passionate about their beliefs and advocates for the change that they want to see, inspiring that desire for change in others.

They're a positive impact influencer who builds followers and attracts expansive coverage for causes they support. Their income generation is in the form of aid, grants, donations, or sponsorship, or through public or aid organisations. They may have some ancillary income sources such as books or paid speaking gigs where they may choose to donate some or all receipts to their chosen charities.

This person is also your public servant, journalist, teacher, lecturer, documentarian working in a space that is there to provide an essential public service. They use their skills to further a common and shared knowledge of matters important to them.

This has been a very legitimate choice of career for people interested in sustainability, considering the groundswell of support for inclusion, sustainable transition, and topics such as climate justice. This individual "lives" the change they advocate for, and as such become positive examples of what's possible. They may also participate in research projects to further support development of the science behind their positions.

❖ *Career Profile 3 - The Lifestyle Influencer*

Lifestyle influencers create impact, not for altruistic causes, but for causes internal to them. They're doing something that they absolutely love and have engineered significant opportunities to earn money from it.

It's not necessarily a traditional career DEAL (Doctor, Engineer, Accountant or Lawyer) - although they can be, it's more something like *"I love surfing, and the way to ensure I can surf more is to become a model for surfing brands and surfing gear, while spending more time on what I absolutely love."*

A singer, cellist, violinist, or pianist may do this work from the sheer joy they derive from performing their craft.

A talk show host like Oprah appears to ds this work because they are incredibly good at empathy and make their guests so comfortable they share more than intended. They can be this effective because of the depth of love they has for that craft.

They found a way to monetise their love for talking to people and to give back as well. This profile is about the life they really want to live, and then finding ways to monetise the living of that lifestyle.

The same applies to the modern-day Instagram influencer who travels the world taking pictures wearing branded items. How brilliant is it to get paid for what you absolutely love doing! It takes time to build however, so before you quit, work on what it takes. Not everything you love doing translates into becoming an influencer in the area, so choose wisely and have a clear strategy if you want to go after it.

The lifestyle influencer will develop one to many relationships in the execution of what they do, so it helps them to be engaging and skilled at communication. As a career, this can be a very productive side gig or a full-fledged job.

Where in your life are you currently playing such a role, and can you do something to amplify your impact from it, earn an income from it, or get better at growing and scaling it?

❖ *Career Profile 4 - The Corporate Jetsetter*

The corporate jetsetter isn't ever going to be the CEO. They will craft a career of phenomenal longevity where they certainly rise to seniority and significance in the organisation (public or private) but will seldom be known outside of that organisation except in small niche circles. The best international example of this personality is Apple's prolific and patented head of design. You may not know his name, but you surely know his work.

If you know anything about Apple behind the scenes in the early 2000s, you know that this character was the brain behind the design. He worked closely with Apple's leading man and is formally credited on the IP patent applications with much of the great innovations the company produced at that time. He saw them move from near bankruptcy to one of the most important tech companies in the world. He retired from Apple and today sits on many boards and if you're pursuing a career in design maybe you know about him. For the rest of us, not so much. Write to me if you know who he is!

Choosing the path of a corporate jetsetter can certainly be a path to self-actualisation and income. It's also likely to result in anonymity outside of a niche. If you want to have a strong personal brand while following the corporate jet-setter path, then networking outside of your company becomes of crucial strategic importance to you, as well as considering moving around to other companies. However, staying in one place and rising to the board level is certainly an outstanding achievement for anyone.

❖ *Career Profile 5 - The Serial Entrepreneur*

Elon Musk comes to mind. Someone who continuously challenges the status quo and our understanding of what can and cannot be done, and potentially what's legal too. That's the kind of personality trait that thrives as an entrepreneur in my experience.

Being willing to push limits with guts, courage, and determination, to learn quickly from failure and continue to take risks, while converting on the major opportunities.

The serial entrepreneur will start several different ventures in their life. They possibly will not be the best at operationally running them. Yet they will definitely be there for all the ideas and direction.

We need this force of nature to take our thinking further, although change at the sort of scale Elon is making comes at great risks and cost. Space travel to create an alternative to earth is still, to me, not realistic in the timeframe we have, but I'm quite sure what I think doesn't matter to him!

❖ *Career Profile 6 - The Corporation Builder*

Bill Gates is the image I conjure up here. Building a corporation that continuously reinvents itself and remains relevant at every glance toward the future. When you look at the legacy, this character built the type of organisation that lasts. Organisations that will take the lead on climate change. Organisations with significant mass market appeal tend to attract more wealth and more responsibility in the eyes of a population and building a company that stands up to this scrutiny and leads change is admirable.

We need people who can build and sustain corporations that strive to be inclusive and future relevant, tackling the significant challenges of AI and other important topics in the public discourse. To become the Fortune 500 or FTSE 250 CEO, you need the long lens of change, trends and understanding to anticipate and guide your firm through evolution and discovery. Is this what you're built to do?

❖ Career Profile 7 - The Investment Manager

Warren Buffet comes to mind, but not exclusively, there are many varieties of investor, some with noble underlying philosophies and some without them.

The key to the investment manager profile is to be someone who takes an opportunity from what capitalism has created in terms of capital markets and exploits that for gain. This can start with day trading, in the form of forex trading, foreign exchange, stocks and bonds trading, bitcoin mining, NFTs, and evolve into buying and selling companies, operating, and managing financial institutions, and brokering large deals.

You can be an investment manager and still do any of the other career types. You can actively day trade, but this can be demanding from a time perspective. You can be passive - set it and forget it for a more long-term return structure, or you could hire fund managers either through a tax-free ISA (individual savings account) or through a normal money market product managed by an approved financial institution. Of course, this is not investment advice, this is just career advice!

Each one of us has an investment portfolio of some type based on the types of things we spend our money on. We can invest in ourselves and our wellbeing in the form of experiences (and the hope is that you are happier for it!), or you can also invest in physical assets which may or may not have an after sales or second-hand market. Luxury brands often have a good resale value for almost anything - clothing, electronics, accessories. Then there's cars, homes, rooms in homes and appliances all gaining a second-hand market value in the sharing and collaboration economy, there are many ways to get into this space if you have a bit of seed capital to get started.

❖ *Career Profile 8 - The Connector*

The connector is a blend of the influencer and the investor. This is someone who acts as a go-between, introducing sellers to buyers but not necessarily based on something that is about their lifestyle, this is more of an opportunistic approach, when someone finds that they have a natural market of potential customers for a brand or service, and align themselves with that. It's not usually their only business but is something that goes alongside their primary activity.

This can come in the form of amazon drop shipping if you are a store owner, travel agents, affiliate links for software as a service company, or sellers of courses or wellbeing experiences. This is about understanding the people you are coming into contact with, their needs and finding partners that can help solve their problems for a "connector" fee or affiliate income.

This can also tip into MLMs - Multi Level Marketing or Network Marketing as it is sometimes known. Not all MLMs are pyramid schemes; but your best approach would be to find out more about whatever product or service you choose to represent before selling it on to someone else. Ensure you do post sales follow up with people who have bought something based on your recommendation to learn about their experiences. You are now lending your brand and your name to another business. Be sure it's right for you.

❖ *Career Profile 9 - The Freelancer/ Contractor/ Independent Consultant/ Coach*

The freelancer is a specialist of sorts who does the work a traditional employee may do but negotiates the terms of each engagement including but not limited to salary, and chooses his or her own hours, although making themselves available for meetings as required.

Freelancing has risks and benefits. As a specialist, you can often draw a higher price for your services than you would on the job market, and it creates more flexibility on your lifestyle choices. You can incorporate the remote work lifestyle, being located in different countries, while still earning an income with more flexibility.

The risk here is that you will need to dedicate time and/or resources to business development, whether it be through networking, referral schemes, social media, or ads. Post-Covid, we have seen the rise of the freelancer, particularly in marketing, data analytics and visualisation, PR, and sustainability services. Freelancing gets easier as you build an external reputation for the quality of work that you do.

Many people don't make the conscious decision to navigate their career options and the opportunities to run parallel careers. Don't be the many people. Take charge of your power to consciously choose a career path, or paths, that fits with the life you are creating for yourself.

Katherine Ann Byam

Take the ones that appealed to you, and deep dive on them. Flesh out what they could look like for you. And what you'd need each to contribute to have the quality of life and of impact that you want. Then you can decide on a priority, to start structuring your learning journey toward a new future.

A career portfolio can look like:

Corporate jetsetter:

An established career with a recognised brand PLUS

Investment Manager:

A property for rent, or a series of successive house purchases, repairs, and subsequent sales. Stocks and shares traded on the stock exchange PLUS

Serial Entrepreneur:

A hobby or talent traded on the weekends/ downtime, PLUS

Lifestyle Influencer:

A social account that promotes your lifestyle and positive choices, and brands that you associate with that lifestyle.

Mix and match it any way you want! But acknowledge that you have options.

CHAPTER 4

The Constant Learner

Developing a growth and net-positive mindset

"And purpose, it turns out, is attention. It's about human attention. And the people that we meet, and the people that I've met on my entire sort of journey through podcasting and research, the people who are successful and the people who are doing interesting things are the people who are purpose driven. And I really tried to understand that. And I think it lies somewhere in the area of people with purpose and are highly motivated. And people who are highly motivated are really effective learners."

Quote - Chris Pirie Interview on Where Ideas Launch - The Podcast for the Sustainable Innovator Episodes 27 and 28

I genuinely enjoyed this episode with Chris, as we navigated many topics around learning, observing the fringes of society before they become mainstream and of course tapping into the neuroplasticity of our brains. It's well worth a listen.

We must embrace what we could be by evolving who we are.

Katherine Ann Byam

Whether you are the dean of faculty of a university or a top tier CEO, everyone understands that learning is a competitive advantage and has a personal stake in accelerating it.

According to a senior executive at one of the top 10 consultancy firms at a conference I attended hosted by the Harvard Business Review just before lockdown 1.0 in the UK in 2020, Companies previously held a competitive advantage for 8 years over their competitors, but more recent studies have suggested that the timeframe of that advantage has diminished to less than one year. This means that our competitors are able to innovate and change the playing field far more quickly than in the past and it builds up the pressure on learning as a competitive advantage.

From an academic standpoint, the approach of most institutions to solving problems traditionally is to apply research methodology, studying history, conducting experiments, and facilitating peer reviews of new methods and approaches. This way of working has led to many value-added contributions to knowledge, evolution and change and is done at a pace that reasonably suited the requirements of businesses at that time.

To continue with this approach, but eight times faster, presents an opportunity for a new way of thinking and a new source of innovative solutions, as well as a new way to approach research and verification.

Today, corporate, private, and publicly listed actors own a sizeable portion of the major sources of innovation and learning taking place in our world. From space to 5G technologies, to connected devices, bio pharma and other solutions, there has been a shift in who is best placed to provide accelerated learning solutions, and a definite increase in private and public sector collaborations.

Many companies are starting to replace the traditional universities with their own learning curricula, designed specifically for their needs, as they have more means than universities do to adapt the learning and strategies needed for today's market. This is a lot to let sink in. Major change is afoot. If corporate actors are not thinking about stakeholders and maintaining a view on shareholders only, and the role of the state in providing key basic services erodes, we are creating even greater social divides.

We cannot have a conversation about sustainability without a conversation about the social contract. In the postmodernist view, advancements in technology have already led to increased decentralisation, democratisation of knowledge and expansion of insights. Artificially intelligent solutions are using structured and unstructured means of deriving outcomes. Learning has become a game of humans and machines.

Let's bring this back to you.

The active learning revolution

My life and business partner is a self-taught data scientist. I say self-taught, because he doesn't have a university degree in data science, although he holds a master's in engineering from many years ago. He trained himself to demonstrate competence in this area by doing four things that perhaps aren't traditionally considered academic rigour but arguably work better for someone with his depth of business and practical experience.

❖ *The use of independent learning academies.*

He uses a suite of independent learning academies, some with a formal learning path and others that provide answers to specific questions. *Udemy, Coursera* and *Data Camp* form the bulk of his structured or semi-structured learning. Each of the structured modules offers show and tell; theory and a worked example of how this applies in the real world. He predominantly uses video but will also rely on reading blogs to supplement his knowledge. He practises active learning, so that he is simultaneously creating his own version using a relevant data set.

Today, there are innumerable learning academies that offer you the option of free learning just out of interest, or charge an additional fee for a certification, if you need to provide evidence of your learning journey. Some notable ones:

Curated learning Content

Sustainability related learning created by noted professionals in the field.

- GRI - Home (globalreporting.org) for sustainability education)
- UN Learning
- UN SDGs
- Many other free resources on ESG and other related topics.

General Learning

Useful learning on STEAM topics (Science, Technology, Engineering, Arts, and Mathematics) created by universities or other established professionals with specific expertise.

- Coursera (various universities contribute content)
- EDX (Free courses from Harvard, MIT and More)
- Microsoft Learn (or Microsoft Docs)
- Khan Academy (Math & Statistics)
- Hub Spot (Marketing and Sales)

- Google Learning
- Scientific Journals

User Generated Learning Content

Created by users, who can range from professionally educated to tertiary and post graduate levels, or people who've learned a trade through experience, or short courses. Although the quality here can be variable, there are redeeming attributes in that they can be based on lived experiences and tend to be in short formats. All you need is to search for what you want! The most popular sites are:

- Tiktok
- YouTube and Twitch
- Medium
- Udemy (free courses and also courses behind a paywall)
- Themed Facebook Communities

Paywalls

There are also many other sites that offer learning for a simple membership subscription, or through short courses.

- Cambridge Institute for Sustainability Leadership (Short Highly Structured Courses)
- LinkedIn Learning (requires a monthly subscription to the platform, but some free courses are also available)

❖ *Through gamification*

The only reason my partner isn't a Kaggle master, is that he doesn't like posting comments. He regularly achieves a top 5% and higher ranking in competitions on the platform. Kaggle (a google subsidiary) hosts competitions where companies can anonymise their data and make it available to data scientists on their platform, offering rewards for solutions to their current data challenge. The entire process is gamified and often monetised, and competitors often share their code and, so, share their learning. You build social credibility by achieving medals, and rankings.

❖ *Community.*

At the end of a Kaggle competition or other form of social challenge, he submits his work on his GitHub repository. GitHub (a Microsoft subsidiary) is the home of world leading software developers and a great repository of open-sourced code. It is a treasure trove of information for learning, or building upon solutions of others, to solve common problems. It's also social, so you can become known for the quality of your work when displaying your results and worksheets here.

❖ *Purposeful use of social media.*

Using Twitter, my partner has built up a following and a reputation as someone with a keen eye for detail, by entering visualisation challenges often set by a member of the community. They organise themselves using hashtags, public data sets and engaging themes. They each go off on their own, do some activity and then produce a result where the community gets to "vote by likes" on the best interpretation of the data set.

He now has a following of PHDs from fields such as climate science and biology, journalists and economists who rely on meaningful interpretations of data sets and a host of freelancers who leverage his code for their own learning and development.

These four ideas are becoming pervasive in the freelancing world. I'm a part of some brilliant communities on Facebook, one of which I manage, where the community is a strong informal community of practice, where you can ask questions and get answers, ideas, or solutions that help solve challenges as we all learn to make the sustainability transition in our lives and businesses.

In Facebook communities, gamification is also used as a sales social learning and social selling approach. People are given three-to-five-day challenges where they get to experience the insights of the knowledge provider, and leverage learning from the community.

Active Learning that is aimed at solving specific problems is the marriage of attention and intention and leads to positive outcomes for both the learner and beneficiaries of their output. Active learning can help you achieve a state of flow.

Katherine Ann Byam

Passive Learning

I personally hang out in sustainability communities on both LinkedIn and Instagram, and they've also become a great source of learning using images, graphics, blogs, long form, and short form posts. This to me is a form of curated passive learning, often consumed not necessarily at the time of need - usually without an immediate use case but serves the purpose of sparking ideas and creativity. Social media also provides the save for later button allowing you to go back and reference something you once read to leverage the knowledge again more purposefully.

TikTok is emerging as a leader on creative capital; capturing learning in short micro videos which are fun, memorable, and quick to consume. It's even beginning to challenge google as a search engine for some of its users.

Audio has the unique proposition of being both active and passive; you can decide what you are going to tune into actively, but the content itself can be consumed passively.

Clubhouse was all the rave in 2021, although its popularity has now waned somewhat. The format is exciting, as it offers a different proposition to podcasts; Where podcasts are more of a listening exercise, joining a room on clubhouse or other platform that host rooms can be a more active exercise and more spontaneous as listeners can contribute to the overall experience. Audio books are more akin to podcasts but represents some of the longest forms of audio.

This style of learning has obvious benefits – accommodating task switching, although retention rates may be less than when engaged in full active learning, it still plays a key role in cognition and supports the concept of repetition as a mechanism for learning and development.

There is considerable evidence that much more is changing:

- Exponential growth of peer-to-peer content on various sites.

- A growing body of auto-didacts of all ages – people at work or children at home sourcing and consuming learning in the flow of work or of recreation, at a pace that they choose.

- A mindset shift to experiences. People in the workforce at all ages are taking breaks and time outside of corporations and careers to seek fulfilling experiences.

- The structural shift from employee to independents or driving the growth of smaller, more dynamic technology-driven SMEs.

- The explosion of e-learning SAAS (software as a service) solutions for companies, and e-learning content and sites that enable free and direct public consumption (Massive Open Online Courses or MOOCs).

- The proliferation of research in neuroscience endorsing experiential learning and the role of learning in the flow of work.

- The rising demand for flexible work, which permits the possibility of greater life balance and more space for creativity.

We need to embrace the mess! The future human is a systems thinker, or polymath. They'll understand various disciplines, innovate constantly and be open to exploring new ideas and paradigms.

In many ways, education has moved to the free market. Yet, privilege is the curse of the free market.

Economic privilege exists for those who have already amassed vast sums of capital and secured critical resources – e.g., water, arable land). Information asymmetry is high, fed by flawed algorithms designed to reinforce old patterns of thinking. And as we are painfully learning at a global scale; resources are not free. Addressing the free-market imperfections would be a good start for governments wishing to facilitate a smoother learning journey.

Organisational Unicorns

I picked up this term while listening to Brene Brown's podcast dare to lead recently, where she described this character as someone who is not necessarily a Millennial or Gen-Z, but who is absolutely committed to learning adaptation and change and who has accumulated vast experience and trust in the organisation. They are prepared to do what it takes, not afraid to learn in the trenches alongside their teams and are invaluable to the change journey of an organisation.

The interesting thing about people with this talent, is that not every organisation appreciates or understands their skill, the diversity of knowledge they bring to the table, or how to use it, especially when they are still behind the curve on building effective agile operating structures. Under-appreciated organisational unicorns can become well paid freelance professionals who make an impact with the right guidance.

To conclude this chapter, I'd like to throw you a curveball.

"Life is empty and meaningless and the brain doesn't like that."

Katherine Ann Byam

This is a signpost to our continuous quest for meaning, truth, purpose and a deeper why. None of these masters truly exist until we create them; although we spend our lives at times trying to find the answer: in the skies, rivers, and tea leaves. We construct our truth and our meaning. What do you want as the legacy of the truth and meaning you want to create and how will you support that with what you choose to learn about?

Scientists apply the scientific method to uncover truths. Alternative scientists (alchemists, spiritualists, and others) apply meanings that rely on faith more than truth.

We dedicate many resources and efforts toward improving our understanding of the world, the universe, and beyond and these efforts have resulted in new disciplines of study, cures for diseases and modern technology.

Yet is it entirely clear to you why any of it is important? What does it all mean to you? The answer to this question taps into your deep beliefs, goals, and your identity. The message though, is that you choose.

CHAPTER 5

Your Goals Need Conscious Action

How to take action toward your purpose

"You should be far more concerned with your current trajectory than with your current results."

James Clear - Atomic Habits

W hy is it easy to take action on some things and nigh on impossible to move the needle on others? What causes that friction in moving forward?

How you break down a distant goal into micro everyday actions is the root to successful change.

If you're trying to lose weight, a micro action can be what you put in your shopping basket. If you're building toward a 5k or marathon, it's about increasing the daily distance, or pace. If you're starting a business, it may be about those extra hours on research, or by building a social media presence one post a day. If you're working on building a positive impact career, it may be having more courageous moments in a meeting to challenge the status quo at work.

How are you accumulating those mini actions toward what you want to achieve?

The Outcome Wheel ™

I use a framework I call the *Outcome Wheel* ™, where you first examine the goal, you have and the environment realising that goal creates, then do the work to find out what changes are needed in your behaviours, skills, belief systems, value systems and identity to make your goal and environment a reality.

I first learned about these elements from my NLP coaches at Pegasus NLP, then adapted it to suit my needs, into the structure of a wheel.

I use the *Outcome Wheel* ™ to explain the elements that make up who we are, who we were and who we are becoming. At any point in time, you could be driven by one of the elements of the wheel. You can be values led or led by the environment you are in, you could be led by your beliefs, or give in to emotions and instinctive behaviours.

Gaining an understanding of how the above drives your life, will help you align these different masters and have them lead you where you want to go. Here's an example of how I dig into each of these points, using each element of the wheel.

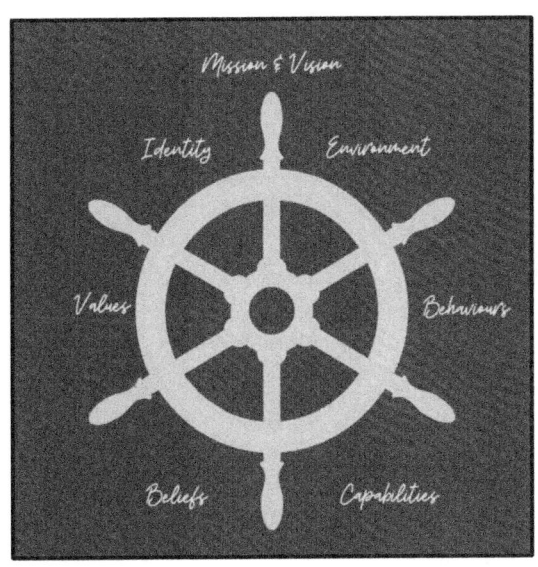

What's driving your wheel?

❖ Mission and Vision

Let's start with the top lever to get into this concept. Your mission and vision are your navigation device or compass. It tells you where north is and gives you a few routes to get there. Your routes may be assessed based on speed, distance, efficiency, but it's not possible to accurately anticipate exactly what conditions you'll find on your way. The mission and vision act as your guide, but all experienced navigators know you need more than a map to access anything worthwhile.

❖ Environment

If your current environment is driving your wheel, you become like a piece of paper or a plastic bag in the wind, you go with the flow. Sometimes you're soaring, sometimes trapped under a tyre, torn, or floating out to sea.

We need some flexibility to adjust to the environment we are in, but to be completely driven by the current environment, you are unlikely to arrive at the destination you set for yourself, unless no destination was the plan all along.

There is another way however to interpret the environment, and that is, to decide what environment you'd like to create, and live in, then actively live as if that environment were already in place.

Let's examine this through a personal example. The environment I've imagined for life within the doughnut, Kate Raworth's articulation of what a realistic goal could look like, appears vastly different from our world today. The future isn't more skyscrapers and fake water features, but a more integrated form of living, with regenerative habitats, a period of control over human birth rates, and efforts to restore animal and forest habitats, as well as protected oceanic zones.

I imagine that we have designed new social, economic, and natural systems that allow us to provide for our basic needs sustainably, as we grow to pursue esteem, self-actualisation and creativity needs with safe exploration of ourselves, the natural world, and the wider universe.

Without making this environment tangible for myself, it's difficult to truly know what it is I'm advocating for, and by stepping into this vision, it may change how I interact with people, and how I reward positive action vs frown upon that which detracts.

If you are going to allow your environment to drive your wheel, let it be an environment you've envisioned and created, and are now bringing to life, rather than any random environment.

❖ Behaviours

After imagining such a James Cameron styled Avatar reality, what do I need to do to make it happen? Other than being someone who believes in the vision, and has values associated with it, what are the key actions I need to be taking?

To understand this in your own context, you might want to run another situational analysis, 6W2H exercise mentioned previously, to understand the context you're in and how you might want to start affecting change.

My specific behaviours are to act as if I'm already having this impact. In the set up and structure of my business, I work toward things like inclusion and fairness in my contracts and business relationships. In the content I put out into the world, I take everyday decisions and infuse them with sustainable principles. I can do more to vet suppliers and customers and incorporate these principles into 100% of my economic activity.

In my personal life I take decisions that lead to minimalism, reducing food waste to zero (I'm almost there) and work on projects that do good i.e., are *net-positive*. I also advocate for change and spend considerable hours on my own education before attempting to educate others.

I've got more to do, however. I still live in a building that does not have optimal solutions for heating. I still generate plastic waste and not all of it can go into recycling. But the vision of the environment I want, calls me to improve on what surrounds me every day.

❖ *Skills*

What capabilities do I need to have in order to go further on my mission and vision?

I learn more about innovation, sustainability, and ethical marketing strategies every day, through formal courses, client engagements, guests on my podcast, documentaries, and other sources.

I put these new learnings into practice in my business development efforts and in executing client plans. The magic questions for me however are:

- How can I make this scalable?
- Is my impact broad enough and deep enough?
- Is the path I'm taking the best path for me?
- What do I need to learn to improve current and future results?

Learning and skill building without clarity on all the other aspects (mission and vision, environment, behaviours, identity, values, and beliefs) can result in broken learning commitments, superficial knowledge accumulation, reduced capacity to focus on areas that can truly make a difference and of course, burnout.

Identity

Your Identity statement walks with you throughout your life if you let it. It's powerful, repeatable, and resonates with who you are or who you've decided to be. It is the deepest place in your psyche, and it can be the most challenging to shift, unless perhaps you think your life is at imminent risk.

When your identity steers your wheel, it can be immensely powerful, a bit like a fully loaded heavy goods vehicle. You are better at driving straight ahead than at turning corners, and most people will get out of your way, rather than try to stop you. You are anchored in the way you see things happening for you and move in the direction your identity dictates.

Your identity statement is also not always helpful to you; it's up to you to decide whether or not yours needs some work.

Let me explain the power of this statement with a personal example.

"I am a black Caribbean female entrepreneur in the United Kingdom"

What's interesting about this statement is isolating what I've identified with and deducing what I haven't identified with.

For those of you who've originated elsewhere but have lived in the UK and have filled out the migration forms, National Health Service forms or any other official documents, you are asked to categorise yourself as some ethnicity, for example black, black Caribbean, mixed, and a few other ethnicities. There is no space on that form to identify as Trinidadian for example and so when I think about describing myself in the UK, I use the terms that are recognised.

I can't explain how this list of identified ethnicities was derived. I'm presuming that many immigrants who live here either classify as:

- Any other White background
- Any other Asian Background

- Any other Black Background
- Any other Mixed-Race Background.

Have a look at the below. We pick up our identities in strange ways, which makes it quite important to be selective about what sticks with us for the long road.

There are 18 identified ethnicities in England and Wales, here they are:

- Asian or Asian British
- Indian
- Pakistani
- Bangladeshi
- Chinese
- Any other Asian background

Black, Black British, Caribbean, or African

- Caribbean
- African
- Any other Black, Black British, or Caribbean background

Mixed or multiple ethnic groups

- White and Black Caribbean
- White and Black African
- White and Asian
- Any other Mixed or multiple ethnic background

White

- English, Welsh, Scottish, Northern Irish, or British
- Irish
- Gypsy or Irish Traveller
- Roma
- Any other White background

Other ethnic groups

- Arab
- Any other ethnic group

In Wales, 'Welsh' is the first option in the White category.

By identifying as Black Caribbean, I'm making a strong "fitting in statement" about myself. I acknowledge that when I mention my country there are people who've never heard about it, so I opt for what's easy, I fit in. There's a lot behind this identity for me, both good and bad, and I won't get into unpacking it here (that's actually the subject of a future book entitled "Designed by Diversity"), but the point is "how you choose to identify yourself matters".

Let's look at the other parts of my identity statement "Female Entrepreneur" and "in the United Kingdom". Identifying as female is an acknowledgment to the fact that there are people who do not identify as the gender they've been assigned at birth. Identifying as an entrepreneur for me is such a strong statement, it makes it harder for me personally to return to any form of paid employment, the word "entrepreneur" is a source of pride. To return to a muggle job (Harry Potter speak for a 9-5), would mean giving up a long sought-after identity and wouldn't be a decision taken lightly.

The statement "in the United Kingdom" is also important. I migrated to England in the United Kingdom, but I've never identified as English.

Where on the first part of my identity statement I sacrificed the word Trinidadian, on the latter part of the statement I've embraced the UK, but not embraced being English. If you look at the racial denominations listed above however, it does not appear as if I could simply identify as British, as it is referred to as "black British" in the sub text above, whereas a white person can be identified as English, Welsh, Scottish, Northern Irish, or British.

Identity matters in how you navigate your world, make decisions, and take action. The identity you assign to yourself, and the ones other people assign to you both matter, to some degree, but the most powerful determinant of the actions you take are the ones you assign to yourself.

Navigating race and bias and all their cousins in the UK is a complex topic that I have to park in order to achieve the messages of this book, but I want to encourage you to choose your identity wisely, and with purpose, this is hardly just about race, it's a statement about who you are, and what that means in the context of how you live your life. At this point in my life, that line; I am a black British female entrepreneur in the UK, is important to the advocacy work that I do.

I am a Black Caribbean female entrepreneur in the United Kingdom with a mission to have a net-positive impact on the communities I'm in and on the planet in which I live. I am guided more by purpose than by profit and want to help create a world where life is safely preserved within the doughnut.

There is a lot more to unpack in this identity statement. What does *net-positive* mean? As previously referenced, it essentially means: does my work help or harm the planet and or society as a whole?

Communities - My dimensions on community are global first and local second, as I operate my business in inclusive and globally relevant spaces and contexts.

The planet on which we live - I am not a fan of space tourism. Space travel aimed at advancing science and earthly solutions can be acceptable, as long as it does not endanger other non-earth life forms, and the earth itself.

Purpose over profit - I will always compromise profit for purpose rather than the other way around.

Life safely preserved in the doughnut - a reference to the work of Kate Raworth, discussed previously.

Beliefs and values

All of the statements above help me bring to life my beliefs and values, as well as my identity. My personal statement suggests some other beliefs about me that haven't been stated explicitly:

- I believe in natural sciences and in the scientific method.

- I value life.

- I value the earth.

- I value people and community.

- There is a necessary trade-off between purpose and profit.

- My actions have an impact.

- I value inclusion.

- I value diversity.

- I believe we can change.

- I believe we can create a safe space for all life.

I recognise all these beliefs and values as essential to my purpose except one; one of them is a limiting belief - I believe that there needs to be a trade-off between purpose and profit. Anything that assumes there needs to be a trade-off is fundamentally limited thinking.

We cannot have infinite growth on a finite planet - that is one of my unspoken beliefs. Yet the universe is known to be expanding outward and can be an unlimited source of resources for us should we master efficient space travel that does not compromise resources. Until we have figured that out however, space travel is an expense of resource we can ill afford.

I have given you an insight into my mind, and how I use four elements of the outcome wheel, Mission and Vision, Identity, Beliefs, and Values. To take action, we need to look at the first three elements of the outcome wheel, the environment, behaviours, and skills.

❖ *Bringing it all together.*

From one identity statement, I was able to drill into many aspects of who I am. This is the gift of understanding this model. You can introspect at regular intervals, and you can use these tools to also understand others, with a bit of conscious listening and attention applied.

The key to moving forward with this is appreciating that at any one point in time, one of the elements of this wheel is steering your direction, positively or negatively. It's up to you to identify which, and how its impacting you.

When your children define you

According to the child poverty action group CPAG, it costs between £160,000 to £195,000 to raise a child to adulthood, the age of 18 in the United Kingdom, the higher number is the cost to a single parent.

That number is stunning no doubt, and that's just until the age of 18. Looking at the numbers above, it's easy to see why many hold on to the way things are; it's almost inevitable that we feel that we need to recoup our investment either on our own or through the success of our own children over time.

The challenge here is that as parents, we tend to seek privileges and advantages for our children. We relocate for their schooling, make personal sacrifices to fulfil their psychological and emotional needs, delay our personal goals so that they may have more choices. When I walk parents through this model, for the vast majority, everything from their identity to their environment revolves around their children.

This is neither wrong nor right, my recommendation is to consider both you, and your commitment and love for your children before you decide on the points of your wheel.

Our current system of economics is a bit like a giant Ponzi scheme, where we take from the system, income, resources, opportunity, leaving the debt to the next generation, which includes our children. We formulate our decisions using economic models built on flawed assumptions, and in order to survive, the process has to keep repeating itself through the behaviours of our children and each successive generation.

We become an integral cog in the wheel of the system, mindlessly moving forward, not realising we are perpetuating everything that was wrong with the past, until we come face to face with the limits to growth conversation that has to be had when you live on a finite planet with a fragile ecosystem in need of rebalancing.

"One thing that economists have got wrong, is pretending that the economic theories and methods are like science, they are pretending that they have actual information. Economists are fulfilling a natural role in human civilisation, the role of the shaman. The fact that there have always been shamans, it's just part of society. It's not wrong that they exist. Leaders have always wanted the comfort of divining you know, what the spirits want, or what the ancestors want, or what the omens are, so it's understandable that the shaman acts as an intermediary with unseen forces. But the economists taking on that shamanic position and claiming to actually know what Wall Street is reacting to or what the markets want, when it is counter to what scientists are warning, that is getting us into a bit of trouble."

Quote: Susan Krumdieck - Episode 72 - Transition Engineering on Where Ideas Launch:

I loved this discussion with Susan. When you have a moment, check out the full episode, but the implications of it are that often we believe in a path dictated to us by greed and not by science, but we've believed in that method for so long, that it's hard to identify that the belief isn't founded in scientific fact.

We desire for our kids more education, more opportunity, more privilege, so we seek to amass generational wealth from which they can live extremely comfortable lives. I assert that it is this thirst for generational wealth that unravels our societies and can create a failed planet for your descendants.

For many, at the end of our turn on this earth, we celebrate that we've done our best for our children, seldom considering at what cost to the planet. Systems thinking, impact assessments and life cycle analyses on our own lives isn't something that most of us consider doing.

Being a grown up for many decades has come with an assumption of working for a business which has almost exclusively profit seeking goals and living a life focused on the pleasure of us and our immediate loved ones. The pursuit of bigger ideals and goals that go beyond the self, tend not to feature in that equation outside of a major crisis. We are now in that crisis. It's code red for the planet.

They say education should teach a person how to think, not what to think. Yet what earns the grades and academic accolades is typically following the script. It's no wonder so many successful and game changing entrepreneurs dropped out of school.

The internet - or world wide web - is in its thirties, and its growth and development over the years has led to a democratisation of information and the creation of meaningful alternatives to a mainstream pattern of thought and education, introducing doubt and providing the breeding ground for more independent thought, ideas, and innovations to rise to our consciousness. Of course, misinformation is a problem, but I'm asserting that misinformation always was a problem. Much of mainstream thinking for decades has been flawed, so it's no wonder we have a crisis of trust on our hands.

In my view the democratisation of information is neither good nor bad; it just is. Being exposed to a kaleidoscope of views and alternatives to our common discourse, is helpful in so far as it promotes critical thinking, and testing, if you've got the energy and desire for it.

Ask yourself this question: are there other ways to secure your child's future than following the same broken path you grew up in?

"Children are THE future, they're not your future. It's an important distinction"

Katherine Ann Byam

We look to our children for legacy. It's the way it's always been done. Yet we are at a time in our planet's evolution, where that connection and legacy will become less relevant. The options for who and what our children will become will change and expand innumerable times before they are adults; and the way they may approach having children of their own will also change. Your responsibility in their life needs to be re-evaluated within the context of either a 1.5-degree warmed earth, or something worse.

CHAPTER 6

The Nine Steps to Positive Impact Career Transitions

B efore we go further into new sections of this book, I want to introduce *The Nine Steps to Positive Impact Career Transitions*.

This Nine step model was conceptualised before the COVID19 pandemic but gained traction and shape as I interviewed and surveyed friends and budding entrepreneurs impacted by the crisis. We cover most of the 9 steps in detail in this book, with further insight available inside my courageous career club programme.

1. Map Out Where You Are

2. Succession Planning

3. Next Role Planning

4. Strategy, Social Media, Network

5. Digital Brand Building

6. Systems and Trends in Your Industry

7. Onboarding and Stakeholders

8. Your Own Systems

9. Pitching Your Ideas for the Next Chapter

The Nine steps follow a certain logic

The first step - *Map Out Where You Are*, is the longest stage of the journey, and is covered by what you've already read in Chapters 1 to 5: or Part 1 of this book. It's the part you have the most control over, and it has the ability to materially influence all the other sections. As pareto goes, this is the 20% that has the 80% impact.

The next 5 steps from *Succession Planning* all the way to Systems and Trends in Your Industry, still maintain some focus on you, but is that version of you contextualised by the society you live in, and the urgent needs of the organisation, your community, your country, your region, or the planet.

The final three steps from onboarding and stakeholders to pitching, explore you in the context of your outcomes and impact. It is how you leverage your purpose through what you do every day, in taking positive and consistent action.

One point to note. I'm a fan of integrating your purpose across work and personal life, but this integration of purpose doesn't necessarily mean that you do not create healthy boundaries between both lived experiences, but more on this topic later.

As models go, this *Nine Step System* will be your master to understand the rest of the book. In Part 3, you will be able to explore your own models in more detail, as well as create new ones, or enhance those that have worked for you in the past.

How often do you give yourself the time and space to weigh your options carefully when it comes to a job, or do you find yourself going through the process of any opportunity presented to you?

When I got started in my career, I took the opportunity that crystalised for me, as I felt I'd run out of options. It's not going to be the same journey for everyone, but I will assert that as we mature and gain experience, that experience should first be processed, before it is allowed to factor in discerning our future choices. Much of that next step decision is shaped by the experiences we've had so far, until we start connecting to what drives us more deeply.

The stereotype suggests that the young are more willing to take risks, but I would proffer that risk taking has less to do with age, and more to do with the size and magnitude of your current commitments and undertakings. Be it student debt, mortgage, family life, or other, we all have a threshold of leverage we're willing to accept and no more, that impacts our appetite for risk.

We will explore the depths of this discussion in the upcoming chapters, but these are the thinking prompts and considerations that will guide you through any transition you need to make throughout the rest of your life, be it a promotion within your organisation, going from employee to entrepreneur, freelancing to employment, employment to contracting, or any pattern of movement that creates a perceptible shift in your life and goals.

I want you to do this with intention. We're spending on average roughly one third of our waking hours at work and possibly more, so it seems sensible that what we do during that time delivers on some of our broader life goals in some way, as that's time you'll not likely have back.

We live our lives at some threshold between joy and pain, challenge and comfort, short term goals and long-term needs. The range of each part of that equation varies person to person. Your ongoing job will be to find and explore your threshold, while honouring your greater intentions.

❖ Step 1 - Map out where you are

Reflect on where you are as an individual, as a contributor and as a professional in your life. Where have you come from, and where are you going? What's your current trajectory? What have you learned about yourself along the way, and how are those lessons contributing to what and who you want to become?

What's critical about this step is the reflection, scoring on a matrix of things you wanted to accomplish or experiences you wanted to have, and then assessing what's next, or what has changed. It requires a reflection on successes and failures, resolved or unresolved work or social hurt, relationships both professional and personal, and their impact on your ego, and longer-term outlook.

This step takes time as all of these notches on our work belt require processing, as they tend to inform and impact our decision making either consciously or not. The more you are able to process the past, the more powerfully you show up in your present - and the more capability you develop to dictate your future.

❖ Step 2 - Succession planning

Once you know you're going to move on from where you are now, it's useful to consider succession. If you are a freelancer currently and you are thinking about moving to a new position or job, what happens to your customers? If you are an employee seeking promotion: who replaces you, and how do you build on your legacy as you take that next step?

This isn't a meeting or career development plan that sits in an HR talent review chart. It's a deeply proactive strategy around what you leave behind and how that serves your future interest and leverage for the changes ahead.

It's also about the relationships that you will need to manage on an ongoing basis or at some specific although yet unknown point in the future. This step can translate into an investment in nurturing a relationship with no immediate tangible benefit, it can be about carving out space for greater inclusion to take shape, or for whatever cause or purpose that holds most meaning to you.

Whether you choose to walk away completely, or develop for the future, make that choice with intention as there will be an impact either way. We will not cover this topic in detail in the book, but this is included in my one-to-one work with participants of my courageous career club.

❖ *Step 3 - Next role planning*

Don't just plan the immediate next job, think long term. To draw on another gaming analogy, I recently watched a programme about Alpha Go, the deep learning algorithm that beat the world's best professional human Go player four games to one. The algorithm could contemplate millions of permutations from the current play, where the world's best player can only manage a fraction of those permutations. Players of GO think several steps ahead, but humans don't have the processing capacity of computers. One redeeming point of mention is that the human won once; because he made a choice the computer didn't expect. Leave some room for randomness, creativity, and unpredictability in your plan as you look ahead, after all, it's only human, but have a direction of travel, that helps you sharpen your focus when needed.

Strategize what's next by looking first at the long term, then mid-term, then the short term. Your immediate next step should be a foundation for what comes next, if you have clarity on the future you want to see. It should consider the skills you need to build for your ultimate goal, the relationships you need to create and carve out, the resources you will need to make the longer term dream a reality. Proactivity and forethought are key at this stage.

The detailed work to do this is supported by resources available on my website. You will however receive great pointers in part two.

❖ *Step 4 - Strategy & execution*

While clarity on what you want to do and why, is part of the battle, how you realise those goals is quite another. If you're not leveraging assets that can amplify your reach and opportunity in new areas, you may find that you remain in one niche for all of your productive time. Niching down isn't by any means a bad thing; becoming the absolute go to expert on some specific discipline can help you to become more known in that space, and help you attract healthier rewards for your work.

This may even help you release time to pursue other interests because you can now choose what you work on as opposed to being selected from a group with competitors for those jobs. Yet even niche opportunities work better if you're able to build meaningful relationships beyond your current geography or context, to expand the pool of potential offers you can get.

How you go about building these relationships can be varied, from networking groups to social events, to conferences, to contributions to magazines etc. It also includes how you build your CV, social profiles and handles, websites, interviews, keynotes, and other outreach strategies.

❖ Step 5 - Digital brand building

Your strategy and execution are amplified if you've invested in building a digital brand. Having a search optimised portal and method for showcasing your talents, skills, and ambitions, helps you reach and connect with people who you can support and value your work ethic and commitment. This is relevant for external moves where your potential employer/ recruiter or client doesn't yet know you.

Digital brand building also has its place in internal moves if the business you work for spans many geographies and industrial niches. The key here is deciding what you want to become an authority on, then backing that up with strategies that are meaningful, sustainable, and convertible toward the goals you have.

❖ Step 6 - Leverage business systems

New and better ways of getting routine things done are constantly evolving and being disrupted. In our hyper optimised technically led environment today. Instead of having a full team of staff to run my consulting firm and other businesses, I am able to work with freelancers and numerous digital solutions to help deliver solutions for operations, marketing, and service delivery, at a fraction of the cost of a full-time employee, and with improved functionalities and best in class service as well.

The same applies to what you are doing today. The rate of acceleration in digital solutions that improve on themselves is so intense today that solutions are becoming cheaper, easier to update and upgrade, and easier to custom fit with citizen developer solutions. Understanding what's changing in your industry outside of your current organisation is essential to bringing real value.

It is also critical to understand and build strategies around what skills to employ or when to outsource, automate, and eliminate. Most of all, it's about knowing where to focus the attention of your teams such that both them and the organisation benefit.

❖ *Step 7 Onboarding and stakeholders*

You've now happily accepted your new role or status and are actively thinking about how to onboard yourself effectively in that job. You will need to build strong systems and processes into this new role or find the common skills that you can integrate into the activities you now perform.

There are three types of personalities when it comes to onboarding that I want to explore for a moment.

The first is the *Mirror*, or *Copycat*, who learns what their predecessor did and does exactly the same. Yet, there is less and less room today for this approach exclusively; everything is changing, evolving, or being disrupted, so actually your fresh and unique perspective can be way more valuable if well developed in certain circumstances.

The second is the *Learner*. Slow to take off in a commanding way but invests time in meticulously learning the technical aspects of the role, so that they can rise to deep competence over time. This character also has its place relative to the role and the context.

The third is the A-*political actor*. This character steps into a new role with a focus on learning the power structures and power dynamics and how things get done. They want to know more about their stakeholders, what their interests are and what they are against, about the ways and paths of decisions in the organisation, about networks of trust, and all the political systems at play, in order to know how to navigate them.

I lean toward encouraging everyone to develop this type of character, even if the other styles are also needed, because this makes you more relevant in your immediate environment, and ultimately more successful and influencing change.

Each role brings its own unique context, deliverables, and mission and perhaps a blend of all three will best serve you.

❖ Step 8 - Your personal systems

What are the things that made you successful in the past and how do they fit into your new working context?

We almost never start with a blank canvas, even when we make radical pivots, although initially and without a process and structure, it may be easy to convince ourselves we are complete imposters. Knowing your own methods, processes, and insights from various experiences, helps you transcend outdated thinking and bring fresh and innovative perspectives.

Documenting your personal systems within the context of the new role is an essential step in bringing your value to the table.

❖ *Step 9 - Making a pitch*

Your success in impact, income and influence are all relative to your ability to sell what you do, or to convince others of the value you create. Any transition will involve a period of figuring things out, and then a period when you'll need to advocate for yourself, your team, or to the wider stakeholder interests. Why should the organisation give you a budget, or increase your budget? Successfully pitching your ideas, projects, initiatives, and actions will define your achievements like no other action, so this may be the most critical part of your first 30-100 days, depending on the role and the needs.

These nine steps are how you design your way to a career with greater intention, purpose, value, and contribution. Part 2 of this book takes us from self to others.

Part 2:

Social, Credible, Responsible

How to become an advocate for change

Clarifying your offer to the world

During the first lockdown in 2020, there was a toilet paper shortage, all around the world apparently. Around the same time, a friend recommended a sustainable provider, *Who Gives a Crap*, as they make their toilet paper from bamboo, which has a much shorter growing time than trees. I investigated the product and made the change. now I promise you I have at least a year's supply stocked in my house!

It got me thinking about what made this offer so attractive. Was it because:

1. The pandemic scared me into thinking that toilet paper could become scarce again, so I didn't want to leave my supply to chance?

2. Bamboo grows quicker than trees and this makes it a more sustainable choice than other virgin paper toilet paper brand choices?

3. It offers 3-ply economy?

4. I wanted to make a statement with the brand choice, to align my brand with that of another sustainable company with great social credentials?

5. They make funny jokes on their wrappers that make you laugh while you're on the crapper?

6. They donate actual toilets to places where indoor plumbing and sanitation is less available, like Haiti?

All of these reasons make up what a brand is, and in hindsight it's difficult to say why I chose them, but I think that I chose them because they are a B Corp with strong credentials and they came recommended, at a time where I didn't mind having a bulk supply in my house.

I stayed with them because the quality is phenomenal, and yes, their packaging makes me giggle.

You have to know what you are in the market to sell, and it needs in some way to link to your desired result, and those of the customer. It's got to be relevant to the causes you advocate for, so there's no confusion about who you are and what you do. This is relevant whether you are employee or freelancer, product or service based. Why should people choose you? What is it about you that's going to be the most appealing to them?

This book will be my first physical product launched into the world. When I sell it, I'm not selling its physics, or even clever mastery of the written word, I'm selling the idea that you can consciously and deliberately impact the world around you with your intentional choices about what you do for work, and life.

You can do more of what matters, with what you do every day for hours on end, not just with a few paper straws, and taking your forever bag to Sainsburys when you go shopping. Before you start branding and marketing thought, let's understand a bit more about what you really do.

CHAPTER 7

What's the point of your job really?

Why should you do what you do?

Does your job matter?

C onfession, I cannot tell you how many times I've had this thought in a moment of frustration in my 20-year corporate career. There were days, weeks, months when I would turn up to work not really knowing why I was there; I did my job, but it all seemed at times to be so disconnected from reality.

That all changed in 2006 when I was introduced to the book *The First 90 Days* by Michael Watkins, the other career transition text I recommend along with my own. This book at the time it was written was a revelation for me. I was already used to self-help and self-coaching, but the book, for its time, was a game changer and it remains on the bestseller list to this day. The gap I've decided to fill with this book is linking our current understanding of climate change and social justice to what we do every day and the role of purpose in business.

What Watkins' book advocates is that you know exactly what type of transition the company is in, so that you know how to adapt the focus of your role. This is a different lens from being centred on what you want and moving to being centred on what the business wants to achieve, and the type of leadership needed to get there. As an example, if the company is cost inefficient and making losses, tough decisions lie ahead on what to spend on, and what to invest in. If it's a start up that just received its series A funding, there's a massive focus on growth and structure.

You need to know the business road map, in order to enhance the context of what you're there to do, not just the role profile and tasks. Businesses change all the time, and perhaps even more rapidly in today's climate so we need to be flexible, but getting the context clear up front puts you ahead of the curve for potentially being an engine of change in the future.

Know what problems you are there to solve and focus your first 90 days on understanding and strategizing solutions for them.

Why does your job exist?

Your job, vocation or service exists for largely three reasons by two dimensions, not all in equal proportion. These are the reasons that most roles exist: revenue generation, cost reduction and risk management. The dimensions that apply to these reasons are short term lens, or a long-term view.

If you can't relate your daily activities to one of these six viewpoints, you have to ask yourself whether or not it's worth booting up your laptop or swiping your access pass at all. These points are relevant to every organisation, although the form and composition may be different.

To create a *"for purpose" and "for-profit" organisation*, I recommend a focus on all six pieces of the puzzle and to know where your unique role contributes to all of them. This will plant the seed of how you can consciously influence change from wherever you stand in the business.

I go into some depth with each dimension and each reason and give some examples of roles that can fit into the context described below. Note that the roles don't necessarily fit only in one box, but the box assigned is significant for that role.

❖ *Revenue generation for the short term.*

- Involved in monthly targets, deployment, retail responsiveness, troubleshooting customer issues.

- *Roles where this is common: retail assistant, delivery drivers, customer service, sales representatives.*

❖ Revenue generation for the long term.

- Involved in innovation, design, customer partnerships, audience building.
- Roles where this is common: *innovation manager, business development manager, partnership manager, social media manager, experience designer, tech developer, talent manager.*

❖ Cost reduction for the short term.

- Involved in continuous improvement, availability, safety stock.
- Roles where this is common: *warehouse manager, security officer, accounts payable and receivable analyst, business support.*

❖ Cost reduction for the long term.

- Involved in innovation, design, supplier partnerships, internal focus.
- Roles where this is common: *supply chain manager, supply chain innovations manager, marketing & operations finance.*

❖ Risk management for the short term.

- Involved in damage control.
- Roles where this is common: *CSR manager, EHS manager, quality control team.*

❖ **Risk management for the long term.**

- Involved in anticipation, prevention & pre-mitigation.

- *Roles where this is common: ESG manager, sustainability manager, finance director, quality manager.*

Every role you can think of fits into one of the combinations above, or perhaps is distributed across all of them.

The Sustainability Conversation

Sustainability, like organisational design, needs to wrap around all the elements of how business is done, impacting strategies around revenue generation, cost management and risk management.

As the metrics and measures around sustainability evolve, it is starting to feature in the results of more job roles. The delivery driver who manages his routes and idle times to minimise cost, delay, and environmental impact, or the warehouse clerk packing boxes or recommending improvements to reduce the use of unnecessary waste materials and augmented pack sizes, or the CEO considering the demands of various stakeholders.

It also affects your marketing and communication practices. Are your messages factual? Unbiased? Promoting sustainable consumption? Are you being inclusive? Are you in any way deceiving your customer in the statements you make and the way you represent the customers you serve?

As far as your management board goes, are they serving the interest of customers? Shareholders? Investors? Communities in which you operate and countries in which your products are sold?

Sustainability is about maintaining systems without further degradation. Whilst this is already an improvement on our current trajectory as humanity on earth, this definition alone may not be enough to satisfy all the interrelated dependencies for our economies and civilisations going forward.

Critical Skills

The above, in theory, is what an organisation buys, and you sell. There are however other factors that may enter the decision process of whether or not you are right for the role, which include, relationships, succession for other roles, team dynamics, changes to the organisational design, and others.

Regardless of the job that you do, there are twelve fundamental skills that we will all need to master to enhance our relevance for the future.

In 2020, I wrote an article for thrive global called the twelve skills you need for an amazing career. I am reproducing that article below, with a few edits to augment my own continuous journey and learning.

❖ 1 - Mindset

Kobe Bryant (RIP) coined the term mamba mentality to represent the work ethic he believed it took for him to be one of the NBA's most successful players. He wasn't born with it. He was known to practise every detail of every skill, watching reels of replays of past performances for hours, to learn how to improve.

Carol Dweck in her book Mindset, discusses the language and perspectives of those with a fixed mindset vs a growth mindset. This is essentially a belief system that high performers have; that they can enhance their performance by learning new things vs others who stop trying for fear of failure.

The brain has the amazing ability to rewire itself with training, due to its amazing neuroplasticity, and it's up to us to continuously develop these learning muscles. In the previous article I wrote on this topic I discussed the growth mindset, but for the purposes of the focus I'd like you to have on this book, I recommend embracing the net-positive mindset - what can I do more of, that helps me achieve my personal goals, my businesses goals, and societies goals?

In general, your mindset opens the door for every other skill to enter.

❖ 2 - Creativity

Something can be made new by a change in its physical state, use or perception. Creativity can be a novel idea, or interpretation, beyond that which was previously known or done within the context that we are in. Another feature of creativity is being able to translate an innovative concept into imagery; a choice of words that conjures up new possibilities and generates value in the mind of others in the room. To cultivate creativity, start by asking "What if…"

What if questioning gives our minds something to go after? A stretch goal? I was listening to Reid Hoffman's podcast in 2019 when I started my business, and I heard an interview he did with Brian Chesky, CEO and Co-Founder of AirBnb. In that Interview Chesky spoke about a brainstorming exercise he did with his team, to imagine what 5-star service would be for AirBnb and then to think bigger, about 7-star, 9-star and what even an 11-star service would be.

That exercise led to some of the most exhilarating experiences being created on AirBnb for guests by their hosts, that far exceeded what you could imagine receiving from hotels.

Setting parameters focuses the mind on providing solutions. Try it with a context relevant to the work that you do!

❖ 3 - Curiosity

A close relative to creativity, curiosity is the questioning skill. It captures the essence of how our children learn and it breaks down borders between people, cultures, abilities. Curiosity enables us to be open to understanding what is different from ourselves. It also serves the purpose of creating reframes, challenging the status quo and extending the ideation time before implementation. Ask questions of others and also importantly of yourself. You may find that you have long-held beliefs that you have not interrogated in a long time.

There are nine questions that I often recommend to my clients that they contextualise when developing the habit:

- What can I learn from this?
- What is this problem or scenario like? Find a metaphor.
- How can I build a bridge with my question?
- How many components does this problem have?
- What's missing?
- How do we measure this?
- What dependencies are there?
- What assumptions have we taken?
- How would this be explained by a different discipline or function?

❖ *4 - Emotional Intelligence (EI)*

Also known as EQ or emotional agility, EI is our ability to recognise and codify emotions within ourselves and others and manage or adjust our behaviours to achieve our goals. (Simple swipe from Wikipedia).

Daniel Goleman's famous book on the topic outlines five critical aspects of EQ:

- developing self-awareness through internal and external interactions,
- regulating your emotions by slowing down your actions,

- exercising empathy "walking a mile in their shoes",

- understanding what motivates and demotivates both self and others,

- engaging and building rapport with others, understanding their perspectives and preferences go a long distance in developing excellent communication skills.

Daniel Kahneman also covers this in his work thinking fast and slow. He discusses the decision-making heuristics we have running in our brain, that may be taking active control when we're being passive. Slow thinking is something we need to train ourselves to deliberately engage, to raise our self-awareness and overall emotional quotient.

❖ 5 - Listening

Excellent communication is largely the product of active listening, and this skill incorporates more than the ear. It involves understanding the choice of words, tone and timber, pitch, of the voice and observing other cues such as body movements and posture. Listening is the job of all the senses.

Active listening links back to our earlier conversation on persuasion, influence, and manipulation. To move others from A to B, we need to understand everything about their state in A, in order to understand how to:

- Modify B, to resemble the most important parts of A

- Build a transition plan that slowly modifies and adapts A until it becomes B

- Don't change at all. If we actively listen, we may find out that A to B should not be the goal at all and there are other levers that can be moved to deliver the same or even better outcome!

❖ *6 - Collaboration and co-opetition*

Co-opetition the combination of co-operation and competition

Excellent collaborators are adaptable to diverse cultures, styles and approaches and can build deep connections and trust even when challenged. Collaborators understand that to achieve their goals; it's better to create a diverse network who share a common goal but may contemplate different paths to accomplish it. They build trust and nurture relationships. It's essential to have a genuine interest in the goals of others when seeking to drive collaborative relationships.

Let's move this into the business context. Competition has long been linked to strategy and to winning, in a zero-sum win/lose playing field. The world still has a chance for us to play the game differently if we want to follow Simon Sinek's model of playing the infinite game. Coopetition as a model has gained in prevalence, through joint ventures and public interest groups, aiming to pool minds to solve major problems.

Tesla famously released its battery technology to promote the development and deployment of more electric cars and to foster the development of infrastructure and networks needed for these cars to become more mainstream. It was in Tesla's interest to release their patents, but it was also in the community interest.

The growth of the sharing economy is an example of how service improvement and sustainable goals can be achieved through a shift in mindset. Last week, I booked a ride from my local taxi company using the Uber App - it was a "luxury service" to be sure because it was more expensive to do this, but the convenience made it appealing at that moment as there were no Uber cabs available. Rideshare apps, Zip cars, the growth of rent-not-buy and second-hand markets are all ways to foster collaborations on individual and corporate levels. Shifting your philosophies of strategy and competition can have tangible net-positive impact.

In the book Tools and Weapons, Brad Smith, Head of Legal at Microsoft, discusses how Microsoft aims to get the other tech giants to collaborate on a code of ethics around the use of data, the design of algorithms, and other areas where there is currently no law, because the private sector is leading the way on its development. Some big tech companies, however, have not agreed to collaborate or jointly discuss ways they may want to place ethical lenses on the work that they do. These are not good signs. A redeeming action from Apple to change its policies around privacy and give users more control on their devices for apps such as Facebook and Instagram have been a welcome change in the privacy conversation, but we do need more collaboration from these giants of technology, to facilitate society's best interests, and not just the bottom line of these companies.

❖ 7 - Resilience

A long-misunderstood word. The most intriguing definition of resilience is that it is about how you recharge, not how you endure, from an HBR Article of 2016. Resilience has, as one of its arches, the idea of self-care; the ability to retreat, rebuild and repair in a regular cycle of expansion and contraction, energy expenditure and recovery.

This skill understands that the mind and the body need to work in unison to deliver the best outcome. Our creativity, energy, and longevity on the task - call it personal sustainability, depends on how well we can create and protect boundaries and nurture our self-care.

Many still align resilience to endurance, and endurance to going continuously without stopping. Before resilience can reclaim its deeper meaning, I think we ought to start branding it self-care instead.

In 2018, I had the first major burnout of my professional career. I retreated to the lake district of Austria for a week and was surprised to discover I was the only "employee" there. It made me realise that entrepreneurs get this. They prioritise their recovery time and restore their energy for the battles ahead, whereas in traditional employed relationships, perhaps (pre-pandemic) was considered a luxury or a weakness. I'm pleased to see the corporate world taking greater steps to embrace wellness and mental well-being. Introducing meditative practices and down time in your routine enables greater longevity and sustained results.

❖ 8 - *Complex Problem Solving*

This skill requires rapid synthesis and sensemaking to distil the critical information for decision making. It requires a strategy for breaking down the problem while drawing from a range of different experiences and knowledge to arrive at a reasoned judgement or decision.

Alternatively, it requires leveraging the strengths of others, questioning, and developing new ideas and solutions.

There are several approaches. The first is working from the outcome - starting with the end in mind and leveraging data and the skills in the room to drive to a solution.

Another approach is to define the constraints or outer limits of tools or resources and then to craft a solution within a given context.

To develop complex problem-solving skills and cognitive ability I recommend:

- Regular activity breaks, to perform new, or varied tasks, either as physical challenges or mental ones

- Do volunteering work for causes important to you either online or in your local community, to get a different perspective.

- Take up a creative hobby; like painting, drawing or poetry

- Network with people of interest that you've never worked with before (take up the 100 coffees challenge, and book two slots in your calendar each week to talk to someone new!)

❖ 9 - Influence

We discuss in Chapter 8 the various dimensions of influence. Here I want to tackle it again from the perspective of the activist or advocate. The person of significant influence can enrol others into a vision of the future, in a goal that is greater than self alone, WITHOUT changing that person's underlying values or motivations. Mastering cause-based influence is a skill that calls on a sense of decency, equity, and community existing in most humans, and coaxing that into action for a specific reason at a specific time. It does however rely on the fact that at some basic level there is some common ground to be found, some shared values that can be connected to.

❖ 10 - Mobility

Regardless of the nature of your work, enhancing your physical strength, dexterity and equilibrium enables higher sensory perception of your environment. Pushing yourself to acquire physical capabilities can have a substantial impact on your mental acuity as well, movement in a choreographed way is also thought to offset Alzheimer's and other forms of cognitive decline in later years.

To improve your performance in this regard, I recommend:

- Exploring yoga and meditation
- Taking on challenges; 10Ks or Marathons, Triathlons
- Climb mountains
- Take up sailing, kite surfing or SUP boarding
- Learn to draw, paint, or play a musical instrument
- Ride horses: working with animals gives you a far greater appreciation for non-verbal cues!

❖ *11 - Cognitive Flexibility*

People with cognitive flexibility are able to shift their thinking from one concept to another and even from one context to another rapidly. Some might argue, this skill is about making us more like machines than humans! It embraces other skills such as curiosity and helps to generate the adaptability needed for complex reasoning. This skill requires variety and mental challenges. Problem solving games, watching, or reading about mysteries and visiting spaces where like-minded people are not – can help you develop and hone this skill.

❖ 12 - Business Fluency

Having a strong command of your native language supports the generation of fluency in the context of selling ideas and influencing others. Native-level proficiency in another language also adds a different level of nuance and can enhance one's ability to communicate. Business fluency is no different. To develop business fluency, practice engaging with your audience using the words, turns of phrases and other non-verbal cues they use to communicate. What is the language of your corporate board? What is the language of your ideal client? Business fluency grants you that know, like and trust factor that is needed in making an impact today.

❖ 13 - Authenticity

Here is lucky number thirteen, which is authenticity. The more senior you go, the easier and more important this gets. In some ways, it may feel like it conflicts with skills that require you to step into greater empathy; but the beauty of combining authenticity with all of the more nurturing skills mentioned before, is that in order for you to be truly authentic, it helps if you accept this as a right for other people as well. It is not mutually exclusive to champion authenticity, and to have a high EQ and skills at influence. On the contrary, these skills blend together to create a person with phenomenal gravitas.

CHAPTER 8

Is it persuasion, influence, or manipulation?

How we get others to follow our lead

"*Traditional competition forces us to take on an attitude of winning. A worthy rival inspires us to take on an attitude of improvement. The former focuses our attention on the outcome, the latter focuses our attention on process. That simple shift in perspective immediately changes how we see our own businesses. It is the focus on process and constant improvement that*

helps reveal new skills and boosts resilience. An excessive focus on beating our competition not only gets exhausting over time, it can actually stifle innovation."

Quote from Simon Sinek - *The Infinite game*

R eading between the lines of Simon's work above, I believe the idea is that maybe our direction isn't the only right path, and that the truth can be somewhere between extremes. We need to stay open in order to learn as we grow, what the next best course of action can be.

There's nothing better than this debate over persuasion, influence, and manipulation to get us feeling like a dry martini in need of shaking. The first and most important person you are responsible for changing (persuading, influencing, or manipulating) is you.

It's cliche for a reason because it's true. Your journey to no longer accepting the status quo leads you to want to change (persuade, influence, or manipulate) others. Persuasion, influence, and manipulation all come about by employing the same skill set. None can happen without understanding the person on the other side of you, listening to them, building rapport, engaging them, and then using their words, ideals, desires and possibly even pain points, when getting your points across. From where I'm standing, the only difference among these three words is the intention bchind it.

Persuasion probably has the least bad rep of the three words, followed by influence, and then manipulation. Language matters, and perhaps one of the greatest limitations of English is that there simply isn't sufficient nuance in our vocabulary to express the subtleties of these words on how we build relationships, create impact, and achieve ends that may be net-positive, win-win, or self-serving, win-lose, or even worse, lose-lose.

If you are not a marketing, negotiation, or business development professional, you've probably not faced this ethical dilemma before in your life. If you've watched popular TV shows such as Game of Thrones, Homeland, Money Heist, or Breaking Bad and others, then you've certainly experienced all of these in some way.

Your level of ability to mould and shape the will of others provides you with the following:

- people who will do your bidding for you: whether they do so willingly or under threat depends entirely on the way you approach it,

- people who are the puppet masters to strings they pull on your back. A goal can very respectfully be yin and yang; relationships work better when they go both ways.

Again, we encounter a problem with the English language. The words Leader and Leadership have been, and will continue to be, used for all manner of characters, the authoritarians, the influencers, the messiahs, it's all covered here.

Academics and writers attempt to create some form of distinction between leaders, bosses, and managers, but again, there simply isn't sufficient nuance in our language to make definitions stick. The reality is our societies work because structures of leadership exist, whether they be forces of proverbial good or evil, and even that is subjective, as what I may perceive as good, you may not and vice versa.

In writing this book, I certainly aim to change (persuade, influence, manipulate) you to look at your leadership approach, and infuse it with principles of the good that I see our planet needs. But before I get to the good, I want to illustrate some examples of what I interpret as the bad.

What's love got to do with it?

I'm an intellectually curious person. I consume content from various sources to form my opinions about the world. I don't practise any religion, but I like reading about them. I keep a low profile in politics, only voting when I feel called to vote passionately for something, rather than against it. I have been an avid reader of management theory for decades, as well as enjoyed twenty years of experience in the management trenches so to speak, and I can state unequivocally that in my experience, what inspires strong leadership is deep love.

The question is only: love for what?

Let's get into another story.

This story is summarised from Netflix Explained - Diamonds edition.

A British Imperialist called Cecil Rhodes started DeBeers Diamonds. One of his competitive strategies was to control the market supply so that diamonds could be understood to be rare and as such in high demand.

When the markets crashed in the early 1900s, there was a mass sell-out on the second-hand market, lowering the price for his vast hordes of supplies. He wanted to find a way to stop people trading their diamonds, so he hired a marketing company. That's when the slogan *Diamonds are forever* was born.

I'd like to think that most people value their diamond rings because of the person that gave them to them, so perhaps any perceived scheming on the part of Cecil is mute, but I must ask you, is this a case of persuasion, influence, or manipulation? This marketing campaign: '*diamonds are forever*', is lauded as one of the best the world has ever seen. What are your thoughts?

The company went on to become the biggest diamond company in the world. Part of their marketing dictated that a man should spend 3 months' salary on a good ring, something that became an ingrained standard in the wedding business but baring little relationship to the cost of producing that ring. I know what I think about these strategies, but it's important for you to assess what's meaningful to you.

Many want absolute power to transform society to their liking.

Netflix can be both a bottomless pit and a major source of learning about our world if you've developed your critical thinking chops.

I also watched the series *How to Be a Tyrant*. It's an intriguing and simultaneously disturbing crawl through human psychology, exploring the lives and playbooks of historical dictators such as Adolf Hitler, Idi Amin, Saddam Hussein, Muammar Gaddafi, Joseph Stalin, and Kim Il-sung.

I was utterly struck by how similar I found their playbooks to be, compared to what we get from many in the online digital marketing space today.

❖ *Here's the summary I extracted from the Tyrant's playbook:*

- Set yourself up as the saviour, promising what everyone wants. Be the populist leader, revered and adored by your followers.

- Seize power, with craft and stealth. All is fair in competition and war.

- Control the narrative. Share stories that support the narrative you want and discredit the stories that do not support your message.
- Discredit the competition.
- Eliminate threats. Make examples of people who rise up against you. Show your power to all that can see, so that everyone avoids repeating the mistakes of the martyrs.

❖ *Have you ever faced such a leader?*

I've seen this type of controlling tactic within governments, public companies, private companies, and other organisations. In the commercial world, it's evident in some of the ways products and services are marketed to consumers, how ad suggestions get thrust upon us: telling us if you buy this, or pay for that, you will have all the glory and if you don't you will be sad and alone.

Is this persuasion, influence, or manipulation? One of the best books and then by extension the best documentaries I've enjoyed over the last couple years is *Surveillance Capitalism* – by Shoshana Zuboff, and the *Social Dilemma* documentary that explores the topics that came up in Shoshana's book.

She covers the way big tech uses big data, not just to predict what we will do next, but to take some control over what we do next. Is this persuasion, influence, or manipulation?

❖ *Before you label, ask about the intention.*

I advocate for conscious decision-making and remaining as much as possible in the question on whether a course of action, choice or decision is appropriate or not in the context. I cannot lie to you, being conscious can be exhausting, but it also allows you to stay in the present, keep an open mind and stay curious.

To achieve your goals, this conscious interrogation opens you up to finding solutions that are more inclusive, win-win and *net-positive*.

Lobbying is a form of persuasion, influence, or manipulation. When a pro-rights citizens group does lobby, it's called activism or advocacy. When a corporation lobbies its thought to be influence peddling, with a big swig of cronyism.

When an individual embarks on a sustainable consciousness journey, we don't expect them to give up all meat, or all single use plastic, or all new clothing and items, but we do expect that they try where and whenever possible to make substitutions.

When a corporation develops their CSR offerings and works on parts of their business to make them more sustainable while not working on other parts, we say that they are greenwashing. As individuals we do hold corporations to a higher standard of performance because they are generating often super normal profits from their non-compliance. These higher standards we set then invoke the cancel culture, and it may mean that we miss an opportunity to collaborate meaningfully with bigger economic actors to support them in faster transitions – and in achieving more net global benefit.

Our human civilisation today is symbiotically dependent on structures of persuasion, influence, or manipulation within our societies. Whether it's political ideology, religion, ethnicity, education, culture, or upbringing, we think the way we do because of the systems and structures in which we live. It takes a great deal of effort to become aware of those influences, and to reshape them within ourselves. I recommend from time to time that you pause to question whether you still agree with the decisions you are making, or with the societal influence around you.

❖ Greta

In March 2019, I was in Queenstown on the South Island of New Zealand. One faithful Friday at the end of my holiday break it happened to be the start of Greta Thunberg's *Fridays for the Future* movement. Children walked out of schools in 2,233 cities around the world, in 128 countries to petition for climate action.

They blocked roads, sang, chanted, carried placards, and demanded governments take responsible action, and stop raiding children's futures by not considering our tomorrows. I was struck by their voices. Being on the street and witnessing this movement was so visceral. I simply couldn't ignore it. What I saw was kids who were not just angry, but who understood a fundamental truth that I had a few years prior opened my eyes to; growth is not inevitable, the way we are going, only decline is.

I had already committed to starting my business with the ethos of sustainability, but that experience really galvanised my actions. Now was that persuasion, influence, or manipulation?

❖ *Let's Brew.*

Brew Dog advertised some alternative beer can options to commemorate the resignation of Boris Johnson. The company successfully uses news and current events in the storyline of their brand so that they can represent their views on social issues and build their brand reputation.

This company has been in the news a lot, for the good that they do, and for the public letter written by former employees that made it to the international news reels. The company is a B Corp and has been working over the years to make their production plants and sites carbon neutral.

From observation, the campaigns on LinkedIn tend to promote the topic of sustainability significantly, despite the period of negative press. Do you feel more inclined to buy from the company understanding the ideas that they invest in championing? Or do you still think it's greenwashing? Is it persuasion, influence, or manipulation?

The takeaway: you need to learn how to leverage communication techniques to achieve your positive impact goals. Some form of influence is relevant to all of us committed to living meaningfully within a society, and we will be assessed as economic and social actors by our impact on the communities around us.

When I trained in Neuro-linguistic programming (NLP) in 2019, it illuminated with great clarity the psychological pathways of toxic office politics, colonialism, and other negative influences. In addition, it also alerted me to many positive postures I can take like self-awareness, self-control, emotional agility, and communicative fluency. I am not a positive psychology coach by choice. I prefer that people be aware of the path of deception, even as they choose to live their lives in a way that allows them to achieve *net-positive* dreams.

You don't get to be net-positive if your frame of reference is your personal happiness only.

Psychology, just like technology, is both a tool to create and a weapon to destroy.

For the rest of this chapter, I'm dropping the words persuasion and manipulation because I think you get what I mean now. From now on, it will be called influence.

You can use the skills of influence to design a more sustainable, fairer, and more equitable planet. You can use the same skills to design experiences oriented to serve your self-interest, or your country's interest, or your ethnicity's interests exclusively at the expense of others.

You can use the influence of technology to solve massive problems in our world, or you can use technology to control people to your selfish will.

This is what I took away from both the tyrant movie and *The Social Dilemma*. Storytelling is our greatest skill of influence. Stories helped us to survive, create legacy, helped countries win wars, helped us understand history in the way the author of the textbook or research intended, and helped us improve our understanding of science exponentially.

Stories are powerful forces. Scientific methods were developed to help us have more faith in the stories we are being told. Stories using these methodologies are by far more reliable than those that do not use any method at all, but no story is impervious to corruption by its host so to speak, so be mindful when others use part truths and false conclusions to sway you. It's important to understand that at any point of this journey through life, you choose, not without consequence, but hopefully well informed.

Psychological tyranny is everywhere, and it's up to us to keep our heads.

We can all benefit from being more self-aware and more emotionally connected, to understand what energies we should support and when to support them.

CHAPTER 9

Money and Wealth

Let's talk about money

I spoke before of a belief I currently hold - there must be some trade-off between purpose and profit and that there cannot be infinite growth in a finite world. Yet making money and making an impact are not binary choices, we can do both every day when we are contributing in any form to the economy, as producer, consumer, or both.

I like watching biopics and seeing inside the glorious lives of fraudsters because it brings you present to thought processes perhaps different from your own. I want to talk about an older programme about a guy everyone knows by the name of Pablo.

Pablo was poor but had a strong business mind on his shoulders and an understanding of economics and capitalism, so he figured out how to lead in the Colombian drug trade. At the peak of his empire, he had so much physical cash that he had a hard time storing it. There is no telling how much of it is still buried, rotted and now unusable - simply out of circulation from his family, the Colombian government, the victims of drug trafficking and the families of loved ones murdered in the trade.

Millions of dollars could be laying waste in a Colombian forest while just next door in Venezuela today so many are suffering to make ends meet.

Money is the quantified valuation we give to goods and services, and in so doing it acts as a medium of exchange. Money made global trade possible, at speeds and volumes we hadn't previously seen.

Prior to printed bills and coins, people used physical assets and living things to denominate value. Cows, fruits, harvest, stones, shells, people. Each of these physical items had their challenges. To be effective for global trade, money had to have the following features:

- **Durability** - can act as a store of wealth over time.

- **Divisibility** - easy to break down into parts and to count.

- **Transferability** or act as a medium of exchange - and this is around trust - we must trust that whatever we are given as money, has and holds, the value we are given.

- **Scarcity** - it must be scarce so that the value can be maintained.

A little history lesson. The US dollar used to be pegged to gold and silver, and via the Bretton Woods agreement, other popular currencies were pegged to the dollar. In 1971 the US delinked its currency to gold and silver, thereby ending the pegged system for the other countries that were a part of the Bretton woods deal, including the UK.

Delinking the stock of money from a physical asset, such as gold and silver, essentially means that we, the citizens of earth, trust that when we exchange services and items for money, that this money will continue to be worth something. Places like Argentina, Zimbabwe and Venezuela understand the risk of this fate in a currency all too well.

We now collectively share a story, that paper money has value, without any hard assets to back up and support that value.

Governments can print as much money as they want to float the economy (they call it monetary policy) and that's essentially what they did to prop up the economy after the Covid19 pandemic.

This has been swiftly followed by inflation as the economies roar back to life.

It is alleged that this ability for governments to print money at will has driven a great deal of the inequality we see globally. It has also funded 20-year wars that solved nothing and has led to continued investment in activities that cause more environmental harm.

❖ *Yet money itself isn't good or bad.*

One of the primary outcomes of COP26 (Conference of the Parties – UN Framework convention on climate change) was to achieve commitment from richer countries who have made a higher consumption and contributions to the CO_2 held in earth's atmosphere to pay reparations to poorer countries who are feeling the brunt of the cost. Leaders from small island developing states (SIDS) such as the honourable Mia Mottley from Barbados spoke vehemently about the code-red situation they face; and that with two degrees of warming in 100 years their countries are likely to disappear under the sea. Allocating funding to support the net-zero or *net-positive* transition that's underway between 2030 and 2050 is an important use of money to do good.

Money earned and used to fund space tourism is a slap in the face to the billions who currently live beneath the poverty line and those facing severe temperatures at the extremes of the ongoing climate crisis.

I want to revisit Pablo for a moment. He used to share his money with the people of Medellin. This was important to him. Yet much of his between $30 to $50 billion dollar fortune, by some estimates, still hasn't been accounted for. Did it go to the people or the rats?

When money gets decoupled from hard assets, you can get the feeling that it is abundant, with this abundance you can purchase anything you want. Yet resources are still finite, which means that the price of resources will naturally climb as that scarcity is factored in and the value of money as a medium of exchange will begin to diminish.

NFTs and bitcoin are gaining status as new mediums of exchange. They are unregulated and lack a robust structure for taxation so that funds can be moved with little accountability and ease.

We are already at the fringe of extremes of climate and social injustice. We need money to live the quality of life we want to lead and to amplify the solutions for the causes that have meaning to us.

❖ How does money flow into or out of an economy?

Let's revisit our economic textbooks for a minute. Money flows through:

- The trade of goods and services locally (circulation within an economy)

- Foreign trade - import and export of goods and services (net inflows or net outflows of money from an economy)

- Changes in monetary policy (adapting the central bank interest rates up or down, changing reserve requirements, and printing new bills)

- Changes in Fiscal policy (Taxation and interest rates, grants, and forms of government funding and projects, investment in housing, health care and infrastructure)

- Foreign direct investment - in the form of facilities, mining, and infrastructure

- Foreign Loans (such as the IMF)

- Illicit trade and the dark economy (via cash, the dark web, and crypto currencies)

As an economic actor with an interest in being *net-positive* and making meaningful and responsible contributions to the communities you are in and businesses you lead, you will need to consider the following:

Am I paying taxes in the economies from which I am drawing revenue?

- Fair taxation for companies operating globally is a hot item on the agenda across the world. In October 2021, 136 countries signed up to an agreement for Multinational Enterprises to be subject to a minimum rate of tax of 15% by 2023. This landmark agreement covers 90% of global GDP and will see 125 billion in taxes being reallocated to the countries in which these revenues have been generated. In the past it would have been an acceptable business response to avoid this agreement by creating new legal entities in jurisdictions outside of this agreement. In today's world where actions of businesses are being highly scrutinised, the responsible action would be to comply, and earlier if possible.

Are my goods and services fairly priced, and adding value?

- Am I delivering consistently on my promises to consumers?

- Are all of my consumers satisfied with their purchase?

- Have I made sufficient effort to deliver the right quality of service?

- Have I treated customers fairly in response to complaints?

- Have I worked to improve the quality of my output over time?

Am I funding positive impact innovations and solutions?

- What innovations am I funding, and how are they contributing to the greater good?

- What causes are important to me and to the business I run?

- What causes are meaningful to the employee base?

- Are my choices equitable and relevant?

This is by no means an exhaustive list of questions, but enough to prompt some introspection and inquiry with any reader, or at least I hope so.

Wealth

I recently visited friends who became parents about two years ago. We were discussing their careers, and what they wanted to achieve, and both parents defined their careers and plans around the life of their new family addition. The father said to me, I want my child to have every privilege!

And I felt my stomach clench up.

That word, privilege, is probably a word any parent would use, as they are guided by instinct to protect this precious life they've brought into the world. Yet that very word, signals an intention to foster sustained inequality and social injustice.

Where our children are concerned, we become tunnel visioned. He is not alone in his thinking. I listen to influencers and entrepreneurial evangelicals on podcasts and in communities online and they constantly espouse about generational wealth. They make statements like you can't help others if you don't help yourself. After you make your millions, you can do all the social projects you want. For now, focus now focus on the wealth.

This get-rich-quick thinking devolves into voting for lower taxes, setting up offshore accounts, implementing tax avoidance schemes and trusts.

Many people subscribe to the Milton Friedman pattern of thought, private actors know better how to allocate resources than governments do. Yet, that's simply not true. The best way to allocate scarce resources is through collaboration and shared knowledge, because no one economic actor holds all the answers.

Many people take jobs and start businesses with income as the primary goal without ever really understanding how the economy works. Rent seeking and profit seeking requires no limits to growth. Except in our current reality there are limits to growth.

I come from a place of privilege when I talk about wealth, because for years I was exactly the same. I stayed in jobs, roles, positions that I knew I was no longer feeling a connection to, and were not *net-positive*, because the money was good, and I liked the lifestyle I could create for myself within it.

I was earning over £100K in cash and benefits a year, driving a company car, and enjoying the frequent flyer lifestyle, visiting my parents in Trinidad and Tobago, or my partner in France. As an entrepreneur today, I don't earn nearly as much, yet I'm still speaking from privilege because I know I've got a decent pension pot invested in a portfolio of stocks, earning 20-25% year-on-year, all legacy from my past net negative job.

I'm not concerned about generational wealth because actually neither my brothers, nor I have had any kids. Any money I accumulate in this life will go to the state, charities I choose or to my partner if he survives me.

I understand the allure of generational wealth, but if it means we consume more resources or endanger more lives with our thirst for accumulating more of it than we really need, then that's not creating a *net-positive* impact.

There is probably a number for everyone, beyond which, you know your wealth accumulation is excessive. What might that number be for you and why?

CHAPTER 10

Your Digital Twin

How to show up credibly and responsibly online

Online and offline

I was out in Winchester UK recently and I met a former colleague, about ten years younger than me. I hadn't seen him in four years. When I say I haven't seen him, he has no digital footprint that could be linked back to the "in real life" version of him. No pictures of kids, travels, job status updates, haircuts, head banging concert events, kid's first poo - absolutely nothing.

He's worked at the same company pretty much since he started working. He's incredibly talented at what he does, and he has skills that the organisation values highly for the future, so my presumption, without asking, is that he has concluded that the only networks he needs are the ones immediately around him and staying off grid is way more beneficial than building his own digital twin.

I start with his example because it flies in the face of everything, I'm about to tell you. I think my friend is committing professional suicide and absolutely missing the point of evolution and change! But to be honest, it doesn't matter what I think. He has chosen what's right for him; however well or ill-informed the choice.

In AI, a digital twin is a simulation of something in real life, that you then use to help model innovative solutions. In my use of the word, a digital twin is a social construct of you, that's meant to represent what you want to be represented.

For some people, their digital twin is a soft brushed, sparkly skin professional and always smiling version of themselves. For others, it's videos of what they did from breakfast to dinner and more. For some it's raw and unfiltered, sometimes up sometimes down but always around. For others it's a highly curated experience. Your digital twin can be anything you want it to be, so choose what speaks to you and your goals the most.

Your network is your net-worth

Whilst it's not entirely true that your network is your net-worth, it bears some merit, particularly in the context of change and transition. If you want to level up in your career, you need sponsors, fans, flag bearers. If you want to get started in business, you need the very same things for investment opportunities and to gain access to stages and platforms upon which to launch. To grow we need networks, so if you are not actively developing yours, it's fair game to conclude you've got a fixed mindset about your growth prospects.

I only understood this as an entrepreneur as it's the first time in my life I held the responsibility for all the moving parts of making a business work. When you are short on time, cash flow and resources, the decision-making heuristics kick in and you inevitably gravitate toward the path of least resistance.

The lessons here are many.

Getting anything through a transition is hard. There've been numerous books written about the famous chasm that most entrepreneurs don't find their way out of. It's the same for you with a career change. Things can get complicated quickly, so it's important to have done the self-work to know what you are about and your own personal red lines.

A digital brand is the representation of your inner and outer worlds acting in harmony; if done well, it inspires people who know you to say yes – I want to be associated with this person because they are true, and it gives people who don't know you the fastest opportunity to assess if they want to affiliate with you too.

Key Personal Brand Principles

- The core fundamentals of who you are remain consistent across mediums, although representation may differ, and it grows with you as you grow.

- It inspires trust - this isn't necessarily trust that means you don't tell lies; it inspires trust in your online version that will act consistently with who you are in real life.

- It evokes emotion, good and bad. Your brand should attract and repel; otherwise, you may be walking the vanilla line.

In essence, your personal digital brand can absolutely become a digital twin; fed with enough parameters and examples, an AI can probably represent you consistently if you wanted it to. There's software like that of course already available. Synchronising your voice, your face, and the way you speak is already a possibility, that's perhaps going to be useful for recruitment inside the metaverse. To get started here, it's important to have clarity on who you want to engage, what appeals to them, while navigating your own authenticity.

It's not just about how you represent yourself, but how you connect as well.

Let's tease this out. Who's in your professional circle at the moment?

The people who come over to yours for a barbecue or a wine-o-clock? How many people are on that list for you?

Most of us need to make greater effort on connection, going deeper and broader. As mycorrhizal networks of fungi are the lifeblood of any forest ecosystem (look this up, it's absolutely fascinating), they represent the same for you. If you are between jobs and gigs, your job is to go deeper with your connections. Reach out and invite people for coffees and teas. Go out to lunch, get on to zoom calls. While you are enjoying career opportunities, go broader, widening the number of connections.

I believe everyone has 30 - 40 minutes every day to do meaningful engagement on the social media drug of their choice. Meaningful engagement means thoughtfully commenting on a piece that resonates with you. Sending a direct message. Creating a reflection of your own.

My Brand Story

The year I became an entrepreneur more than 60% of my LinkedIn network was made up of current or former employees of the company I worked for. I needed to generate new connections that were more socially relevant to the direction of travel I chose.

❖ *This is how I went about it:*

- In person experiences - trade expos

- Speaking in communities

- Joining "social courses" - live taught events that bring people together in one digital experience

❖ The keys to building a network through these sources are:

1. Connecting/following relevant keynote speakers on socials and interacting meaningfully with their content on a consistent basis.

2. Exchanging social media handles with participants, virtually or in person. Attending a few selective *meet and greet* sessions where they are offered.

3. Represent your idea as a keynote speaker to attract an audience and followers who you can interact with to further develop your idea for the future.

❖ Online communities

A well-managed Facebook group on a specific topic of interest is a rare but brilliant resource. A targeted and focussed group which has high interaction and engagement from participants is golden and serves many purposes. A group that has inspired me like this is Women in Marketing - at the time of writing they are well over 50K members, and the content is all user generated and participative, with little to no spam (I know right! A marketing group with no spam!). It has evolved into a real community of practice for salaried marketers, freelancers, and business strategists. I'm proud to be connected with the owner of this group.

Another example is the group Sustainable Living, with well over 130K people, it is a community of practice on how to make sustainable swaps in your life. I'm also in regular contact with the owner of this group.

Another example is my own community of *Women in Sustainable Business* - a group of more than 4000 members. It brings together freelancers, coaches, product-based sellers, consultants, and consumers interested in making a meaningful pivot, growing their sustainable led - business or trouble shooting problems and ethical dilemmas. Being a conscious business is not easy, as it's not really been done consistently before now. So having a supportive community is everything.

A skilfully curated social feed will help you raise your knowledge and expand and deepen your knowledge, for the cost of converting unstructured social media scrolling to intentional and mindful engagement. Think about it, you do have the time, it's a matter of intention and strategy more than time usually. Choose wisely for your circumstances.

❖ *Social media bubbles*

In general, I think that social media bubbles are dangerous and foster group think over creativity; yet strong communities of practice break the negative potential effects. I'm in social media bubbles and communities of practice on Instagram and LinkedIn to a point; I have many like-minded followers who engage with my podcast and deep reflections on the journey toward *net positive*. Yet I'm pleased that I still use the platform to connect with people from my past and to follow up on other intellectual interests, so I can deliberately engage in new circles.

I've built an organic following on LinkedIn by meaningfully engaging on content in my zone of genius and also colouring outside the lines of that; sharing thoughts and opinions on topics such as the metaverse, diversity equity and inclusion, change management and data science. From a brand perspective, I position myself as a polymath with a keen interest in sustainability.

What could this social brand building look like for you?

CHAPTER 11

Busting HR Myths

Improving the Human Resource Management landscape

My life and HR

A while back, a friend (perhaps a former friend?) disconnected with me on LinkedIn. I noticed that she'd viewed my profile and that she was no longer connected, so I reached out to her. She explained that she didn't appreciate my anti-HR content and didn't need to see that stuff continuously on her news feed. My friend works in HR, and I use my platform at times to call out the ways HR is failing both employees and employers and what they can do about it. This is another example of choices being made.

What went wrong with HR over the years? - The answer; Milton Friedman, Jack Welsh, and shareholder capitalism. If you want me to expand on this, reach out to me on LinkedIn and let's start a conversation.

I am going to review some of the practices I've experienced in the context of HR and critique them toward a view of perhaps not HR bashing as I know it can come across, but problem solving. A poorly managed and executed HR function can have a disastrous impact on an organisation's performance.

Recruitment and ATS tracking

HR ATS systems screen candidates for fit. Job titles, relevant past experience, key words. This type of screening eliminates creative and curious candidates, or forces them to make fundamental changes to their CVs in order to fit in.

We lose precious talent and creative people from the workforce every year due to these rigid, computerised metered ways that we manage recruitment processes. Yet the process today does save time.

This reminds me of a false economy, where businesses reduce the cost of the recruitment process as much as possible and hire for fit. The risk is that in the long term, you are less innovative, less creative, and irrelevant to a rapidly emerging green, and or diverse economy.

This is a topic of deep personal significance to me. I've aborted so many job applications, because I haven't felt that my CV fit, and I'm not inspired to make it fit. Most humans reading my experience are intrigued and most clients who benefit from my broad experience find me insightful. It's difficult to communicate those values via a keyword tracker.

I've been an entrepreneur for over three years. Recently a friend of mine who works at one of the *Big* 5 tech companies invited me to share my CV with him, because he thought that I could make a difference there.

I considered it. Long and hard. My CV is not designed for applications to full time employment anymore, it's more oriented to presenting to prospective clients for my consulting gigs. I hired someone to have a look at my CV (you know the story about the cobbler's shoes, right?) because over the life of my career, I haven't been building toward being a corporate jetsetter, I've been building toward entrepreneurship and therefore it's difficult to build one coherent story for a non-generalist role.

I started in finance, as I completed a professional chartered certificate in accounting fresh out of high school. After eight years of doing every finance role available to me at the time, I moved into internal audit, where I spent the next five years travelling the world, auditing every business process from marketing, HR, Finance, IT, Operations and Corporate Social Responsibility. I then moved into the supply chain and took on the responsibilities of risk management, project management, change management and capability development over the next seven years.

During that time, I also completed an MBA with specialisation in Innovation Management. In 2019, I started consulting on digital transformation projects partnering with my former CIO turned data scientist business and life partner and started studies with Cambridge Institute of Sustainable Leadership on Sustainability and University of California Berkeley Law on ESG.

My CV adviser spent three weeks with my CV, then told me she couldn't do it. She didn't feel like she had enough experience to create a coherent story from my fruit punch CV. It was an important experience for me because it got me reflecting on: what's the role of HR in recruiting talent?

My CV has never passed through an automated tracking system and come out the other side on top. My jobs and opportunities have all come from my network, because it's easier to see the thirteen skills I mentioned above when you look at a CV like mine with so much variety, than it is to see strong and deep technical experience in any one discipline.

HR like other functions across the business, has had to turn their focus toward efficiency and not effectiveness in the talent process. The introduction of ATS trackers and key word searches that look backward more than they look forward, has built in biases in the recruitment process. A CV like mine that to a human eye communicates a deep and broad set of human skills would never reach the desk of a prospective employer, without going outside of the system.

To successfully be called to an interview via an automated tracking system today, it's all about keyword optimisation and retrofitting your CV to meet the stated requirements of the job and nothing else.

To HR and to you as a current or future hiring manager, I recommend scrapping CVs and hiring based on digitally constructed and gamified challenges instead. Challenges provide insight on how individuals work under pressure, collaborate, and shines a light on their knowledge and ability to repurpose knowledge. It's also key consider what additions the existing team needs, when shortlisting prospective candidates. CVs are too blunt instruments in an age where creativity and a host of other "power skills" hold more sway.

One way to manage such a recruitment process is via hackathons, digitised games, interactive games, play offs, and team events. These tools have been used by companies such as L'Oréal and PWC with remarkable success.

Jobs seeking culture fit

The problem with a culture fit is that it is exactly the opposite of Diversity and Inclusion. A culture fit in practice means that we all look different but behave the same. It is why women are told to lean in, wear pants suits, become alphas and be business dragons to get promoted, as opposed to being their authentic selves. It is why certain feminine traits are seen as weak in business and are mocked, teased, and negatively perceived in talent review sessions (true talk).

Hiring for culture fit is a key contributor to why change is so difficult in larger organisations, and why they currently face a nightmare to adapt and pivot quickly. It is also a contributor to why people leave; should people grow and become someone else, they often struggle to find themselves relevant in a cultural dynamic that largely stays the same.

Culture fit is attractive because it is convenient to lean systems. The more homogeneous we are, the more we can reproduce the same results is the theory. A friend of mine, Felicio Ferraz, Founder of Leader's Talk, once reframed an age-old quote: *To do the **same thing** and expect the **same result** is actually crazy in our modern world.*

Lean systems worked when we operated under outdated economic principles in the context of continuous growth and abundant resources. Today in the 2020s, we have less than a decade to redesign all our models and our economics to consider not just scarce resources, but social impact, limits to growth, income inequality and corrupted political systems.

HR gets the bad reputation for executing poor policy, yet the responsibility does sit here, as HR like all other functions requires a strategic dimension, looking long term at the implications of different operating systems and cultures on the firm's potential.

Instead of culture fit, HR needs to examine culture add. How can we add new dimensions, perspectives, and belief systems to our culture to help us see unique solutions to sticky business, community, and planetary problems?

I interviewed Tessa Clarke, CEO and Co-Founder of Olio, the food sharing app, and she and her co-founder Sassha have embraced culture add across race, gender, neurodiversity, and training, to build their team. This is particularly beneficial for organisations committed to continuous innovation. Culture fit can repress employees from speaking up, and challenging the status quo, creating momentum for more tunnel vision.

For leaders, adjusting to culture add requires a few core things to be in place. Strong self-leadership, a clear understanding of the company's purpose, and a robust system of learning.

Management vs Leadership

The principles of agile teams and sprints have been around within the IT and product development spaces for decades and over the last decade these foundations have been applied with more frequency to other functions throughout a business.

The roles in agile teams tend to be less about management and more about facilitation. Based on what I could find on search however, these changes still have not created a wide scale change in job titles throughout organisations.

I did a search for vacant jobs with the word Manager in their title in the UK on LinkedIn. I got 278K plus results. The word facilitator had 3.4K results. The word coach - 25K results.

I narrowed my search to have a look at this in some of the world's leading companies. GAMMA and some of the world's top consultancies still actively recruit managers when the post roles; as opposed to leaders, team leads or coaches.

Words matter. Frederick Taylor was the first to introduce management theory in 1909, during the age of the second industrial revolution. His theories were based on simplifying work and having a division of labour such that work could be repeatedly and consistently executed with greater precision and efficiency. A manager's job was in monitoring employee performance of tasks assigned.

This is still largely the way we think about management even though we are now into the 4th industrial revolution, where roles for humans are becoming more analytical and more creative. The application of science to management has brought about the reduced need for management, yet organisations are still late to adapt.

What then is leadership? Leadership is the successful architecture and modelling of an organisation's narrative. It requires an understanding of the environment the organisation wants to create and behaviours that give rise to such an environment. The leader actively identifies the skills needed by the teams toward the ends of the narrative and taps into the values and beliefs necessary as a fertile ground for the narrative to be effective.

Leadership is less about the task and more about the thought process behind the task and overall intended performance. Where leadership is strong, there is less need for control, as the fertile ground created facilitates the intended performance.

During the Pandemic of 2020 this idea got tested as much of the business world moved to remote working. This was a successful experiment for some companies, while others were quick to reverse the decision once legal restrictions were removed.

I'm going to speak from personal experience on this. I've found working with freelancers to be delightful as a change from traditional management; freelancers are naturally driven by their results - they tend to know more about their specialist area than I do (a lot more, that's usually why I hire them) and they work flexibly but make themselves available when needed most.

I decided to compare this to my past experiences in big corporate and I found these to be the reasons that freelancers I've worked with have been such brilliant examples of the potential of remote and flexible working.

- They tend to work on missions. Most freelancers adopt a niche, and a set of ethos, then work toward finding customers who resonate with them personally. They work with strong brands/ or strong personalities behind the brands - leaders who have a great narrative around what they do.

- They agree on performance objectives at the start and it's usually a collaborative process; they are respected for their input on what's realistic and what's a stretch.

- They plan ahead, and work to deadlines, but not on a schedule. They get to choose how their work fits around their lives and not the other way around.

Observing this, many companies can make effective use of learning from the fringes to steal a phrase from Rita McGrath, lecturer at Columbia University in her book Seeing around Corners.

Amazon and Jeff Bezos are famous for the idea of being a day one company, embracing the culture of the start-up in continuous learning, flexibility and taking some risks. Yet acting like a start up as a principle isn't recommended for every situation. How do we then differentiate when we need a manager vs when we need something else?

I like the work of Alexander Osterwalder in his book the invincible company to explore this topic in more detail. He talks about two organisations in one, where each organisation has a unique focus, one for explore and one for exploit. Exploit is where you need your managers. Lean, fast, continuous but iterative improvements. Explore is where you need team leads, visionaries, sponsors, testers, ambassadors, developers, roles that involve far more participation and interaction.

There's no doubt that the role of traditional management is on its way out for organisations, as systems get leaner, more efficient, and more automated. HR's role in this is in reshaping the organisational design. How many organisations do you know are set up to encourage and actively facilitate innovation by their org structures? HR needs to play a bigger hand in re-examining the roles of hierarchies and matrixes as we develop the future organisation.

Reward structures based on the market

HR reward structures communicate a strong message to people about their value to the organisation. Where executive pay is so far removed from the salaries of those customer-facing, it sends a message that is hardly particularly well explained or justified.

Interestingly the few places that I seldom see this level of disparity is in start-ups. In start-ups that are strapped for cash, people are rewarded by seeing their purpose come to fruition, and often in shares that offer a promise of income into the future. Many times, founders and owners forgo their incomes to accommodate their teams, because they know how important it is to have skilled and effective resources designing the vision they have for the future of their companies.

The distortion happens after the company has grown and scaled and invited VC backed funding. Then the traditional shareholder capitalism takes effect. HR in this case largely follows the market as a guide. In times of momentous change, following the average of the market is not what leading organisations do, instead they rewrite the formula. I've discussed Brew Dog's example in an earlier chapter, but I want to reference them again below.

In May 2022, Brew Dog's James Watts announced that they are now an employee and community owned company. He shared that all his bars now share roughly 50% of their profits with the amazing people who work there and the community of crowdfund investors who supported their initial growth. This is a powerful demonstration in aligning actions, values, and rewards.

Other companies are discussing having employee representation on boards, and board committees to look at entire compensation packages, not just board compensation. Much is set to change in this landscape.

There's no easy answer to this when you are literally re-inventing the wheel, but this is another area that requires more innovation and strategic foresight from HR. My recommendation is to review this growing trend and follow suit.

Part 3:

Jump, But Know How to Land

The First 90 Days

F or some, this is where the career strategy begins. There's no denying that this is fundamental and needs strategy but developing that strategy without the two sections that came before is a recipe for painfully sustaining business as usual toward some dangerous consequences.

The good news is that we are problem solvers. We are people who are armed with tools, mental models, and frameworks to break down the problems facing businesses in becoming more responsible actors while still profit seeking. We are emotionally intelligent and more versed on complexity than we have been before.

Your new career opportunity would likely have brought with it a change in your personal economics as well, with your monthly income going either up or down, becoming more or less consistent, or requiring more close management depending on the path you chose. It's important to start the ball rolling with getting your head around that and intentionally reviewing any potential impact on how you manage your own life.

This isn't financial advice, but I recommend becoming someone who actively manages the assets and liabilities of their life. For the past twenty years, I've been managing spreadsheets of inflows and outflows, tracking my investments, and making timed strategic decisions about these, related to my goals and vision for the future. Both as an employee and an entrepreneur, I've found this financial health to be an essential cornerstone to future action. This isn't obsessing about a magical number, but it is understanding what needs to shift or change in order to achieve a goal which depends on your finances, as let's face it many goals do.

The next critical review that should happen at this stage is deciding who you are in this new role or capacity. I advocate for both authenticity and understanding the context you are in, and I believe this is essential pre-work to starting something new. Who do you need to be to achieve your goals in this new context? It's time to revisit the *Outcome Wheel* in Chapter 5, before moving forward with your plans.

The third and final review I'd suggest is thinking about what's next in your timeline toward the future you. What would the version of you that's sitting three to five years ahead most need from present you in this new context, to be successful?

Contemplating these questions are the foundation of your strategies as you assume your new job. Get your journals out, and work on these questions.

CHAPTER 12

Onboarding

Navigating your new job

Power dynamics

W hat frustrates you the most when you're in the position of having to train someone new? Think about it, because the answer to that question gives you clues about your technical strengths, your power skills, and the nuances of how decisions are made in the present context you're in.

Following a process isn't hard. Knowing how to technically calculate a stock policy, or validate a cash flow statement, or analyse a variance, may require some knowledge about the business, and some clarity on assumptions, some insights about history and future plans and projects, yet they are still processes.

What's really interesting for you as a new team member is to go deeper into the dynamics of power, decision making and narrative creation in the new setting you are in. This is relevant if you've changed management levels, departments, regions, or companies – every context has its pulse and your goal during onboarding is to sense that pulse.

You will want to uncover which change programmes have been successful in the past, which projects failed, and why. It's also beneficial to understand how your predecessor was perceived by peers, seniors, and direct reports, to understand the expectations and their gap from the role you've agreed to do, as well as the gaps you may discover between the role profiles of your teams and what they actually do.

You will need an appreciation of the appetite of that team, department or organisation to innovation, agile work methods, matrix structures, creativity, and inclusion.

Getting this insight early on is the surest way to set up for success, and is essential to get ahead of, within your first thirty days on the job. Integrating technical aspects will certainly become more important later, but these strategic points will help you design a better transition plan for the rest of your 90-100 days integration strategy.

To get these insights, you need to skilfully craft your questions to elicit authentic responses, which includes adapting the setting and context, asking open ended and clarifying questions. You will also need to do this exploration without judgement; suspending your own rules and value statements until you've arrived at a sufficient depth of understanding.

A guideline for constructing your onboarding plan

❖ *1 - Request a pre-read pack that includes having a complete view of the business.*

Get insight on the organisational design, your complete role profile and those of your direct line manager and your direct reports. If you are in employment, freelancing or contracting, this is just as useful.

Know the department or business unit's current level of success, its contribution to the wider organisation in terms of revenue, costs and risks in the short term and long term. This requires prior year annual reports – if publicly listed, any performance reports produced in the last three to six months and a view of the business plan. Knowing your budget and its current allocation is also useful.

❖ *2 - Break your role down into key processes and key relationships*

When accepting a new role as an experienced professional, you already have some clear ideas about what processes and relationships you would expect to find so document them. This allows you to challenge these preconceived processes and methods during your onboarding.

It's also helpful to consider what will help you most to get going on what you consider to be the first priority – or if you're unclear about what that is, it gives you some of the language you'll need to find out.

❖ *3 - Engage early, socially*

We spoke about your digital twin before. Most people have some form of social identity; Some combination of a LinkedIn profile, Facebook, Instagram, Twitter, Tik-Tok, Snap Chat, YouTube, Twitch, WeChat, Weibo, and others. Know who you'll be working with, do your profile research, as it can help you ask more human questions when you first meet.

Depending on the person's proximity to your role, you may wish to connect and or socially engage with publicly available posts, or invite for an informal virtual tea or coffee, or in person if proximity permits. Your objective here is to break down barriers and start with warm interactions as you build toward strong working relationships.

❖ *4 - Do some unstructured ethnography*

Let the earlier parts of your induction program be unstructured and almost ethnographic studies of how things work in the organisation. The idea here is to identify the following:

- **Change Unicorns** - Assets long standing in the organisation with significant depth and history, a strong following, and a willingness to learn. These are people who will be key to the success of your programmes and will need to be of priority focus for you.

- **Conflicting Agendas** - To successfully run an organisation, some things at times will need to be sub-optimised in order for a higher priority to be optimised. There are organisations who are capable of using their internal data to map out exactly what levels of sub-optimisations are appropriate where and embed that in their processes. Most organisations however are not that evolved and as such you may notice this conflict playing out in relationships between functions. Observe and learn.

❖ 5 - Map things out

Mind maps and process flow charts using paper - free hand as you do your walk throughs go a long way in detecting and addressing any gaps that may exist - either in the process or in your understanding of it.

Ask questions of yourself such as – *What is the intention of this part of the process? Is that intention being fulfilled? What's its impact on other important processes?*

❖ 6 - Don't take action before the time is right

It's tempting to go through an onboarding process and want to change things that appear to be glaringly wrong. Resist that urges and remain for as long as possible in the question. Much career transition advice talks about getting early wins, and you will need these, but early wins should not come at extreme mid- and long-term costs. Instead, give yourself a tight timeframe to work out the processes and organisational dynamics in effect, then list all the opportunities you found in a decision matrix to help you prioritise the right early win - lining up your dominos appropriately is more crucial than knocking the first one over.

❖ 7 - Create a stakeholder map

Mapping your stakeholders both internal and external and developing strategies to address the critical ones is essential in the context of not being able to do everything. The further you go in management and leadership the more essential this is to progress, performance and boundary setting. In the context of sustainability, stakeholder maps have become more crucial and have taken on significantly broader external contexts. This is worth a collaborative exercise with both your team and your predecessor before you begin executing against it. I cover this in far more detail in my course and in my one-to-one coaching work.

CHAPTER 13

Habits and Contexts

Creating a compelling personal playbook

Personal systems

We all have personal systems or methods that have resulted in us achieving our goals in the past. It's how you go about understanding problems, testing solutions, and making decisions. For many of us, these personal systems run on autopilot, and are considered *tacit knowledge*, things that are difficult to decode and teach, but reside with you and can be passed on through observation and interaction over time.

I put forward in this section that these thoughts, ideas, and patterns can be documented by you into a personal playbook which can in turn be reviewed, challenged, and improved. It doesn't have to be something elaborate; a notebook you dedicate

If this is your first-time contemplating this, the idea is to start capturing early on, which of your systems will be useful for the new role that you're going to take on. Doing this is useful for preparing your CV, showing up powerfully in interviews and for getting prepared and rapidly assimilating your new role.

To build your personal play book from scratch, it's time to *data mine* your past. Let's start with:

❖ *1 - What are the methods and learnings you have from key successes?*

I start here because it's unnatural to ruminate on past successes; yet it's so fundamental to discovering on a deeper level your strengths, and the context and conditions to find flow, as we discussed in Chapter 2, exercise three on finding flow. What you are looking for here are conditions that existed at the time, the processes you used, the outcomes you had immediately, and the longer-term impact of that work. This will help you to understand how to engineer your environment and systems to deliver on these goals.

❖ *2 - Where have you fallen in the past?*

Looking to our failures for learning in a scientific way, helps us to identify if we have some easy to remedy flaws in our process, or whether or not we have a fundamental gap that needs more time to remedy with training and with practice, or whether those moments were actually communicating something else; for e.g., this activity of x should be outside of my responsibility or remit in this role. That's a valid conclusion too!

With leveraging past failures, it's essential to organise that review into areas of strength that can be further developed and improved, areas of weakness that actually with some knowledge can become strengths and areas of weakness where you only need to achieve some basic level of competence, but you're never really required to be the best.

In this overstimulated busy world, we live in, you can have great intentions about learning everything and execute on nothing because you haven't aligned and focussed on what's most important to you. Choose examples for this exercise that relate as much as possible to the new role you will assume.

❖ *3 - Leveraging mindset with your models*

We often think about mindsets as something permanent; but in practice we adjust our mindsets depending on the task at hand, our past experiences with the current task or situation and how we want to respond.

To explain this, let's use the example of a monthly team meeting. Perhaps many of us show up to these prepared to talk about what we've done over the past month and what we are focussing on toward the next cycle. So, you prepare for that meeting by getting into a reflective space, making notes, and perhaps revisiting past commitments. You're probably thinking about efficiency, securing some recognition, and getting alignment for what's next. What if you were to switch your mindset for the next meeting from reflective and inward focus to, what do my colleagues need from me to be successful?

In practice, this can look like - reflection before the meeting to ensure we are prepared, but attention to others during the meeting to be able to deliver support.

There isn't a single meeting that cannot be improved in this world with some mindful shifts in perception, intention, or attention. I want to invite you to disrupt your meetings for a few weeks by changing your mindset ahead of it.

The same pattern interrupt can work for any task. It requires only an alteration in your mindset however temporary, in order to unlock something, you haven't previously explored!

❖ *4 - Automate the routine*

Where possible, look for the things and practices that you have to find out which areas of your role would be better off with some clever automation and which you think require contextual judgement. In the current climate in which we work and live, the key words are simultaneously disrupt yourself, and reinvent yourself. This helps you to stay focussed on progress while addressing your personal growth potential.

In the resources section of my website, you can find more thinking prompts for developing your own playbook.

CHAPTER 14

How to Create the Perfect Pitch

How to earn funding for your projects and innovations

What's your pitch?

When we get to key stages in our onboarding, let's say 30, 60, 90 days, it's time to step off the fence and start pitching new ideas, backed up by solid intelligence and considered action plans.

We need to think strategically and develop our pitches well, because every action, improvement, and innovation you want to take on, will demand resources in time, or funding and you will be competing with other departments and interests for a limited pool of funding. Projects that you pitch can come from any of the three reasons and two dimensions; revenue, cost, and risk, short term, or long term, and depending on the nature of your role and budget, it may be possible to launch multiple ideas at the same time which may even contradict each other for the purpose of innovation and learning. It's important to know your context and what's essential to getting things done, and or re-prioritised as required.

As you understand the wider organisation and how your role and your team fit within it, this will give insight on what to include in your pitch that may be required to get the necessary buy-in. It's preparation to negotiate what you need, with a clear understanding of alternatives, finding areas for mutual shared benefit and leaving space to understand any challenges or concerns.

You are also going to be interested in using the pitch to get buy-in with your new team, as they will be essential in helping to suss out what's important to them as you look at all the other implications as well.

Essentials of a good pitch

Create a desirable transformation. Whether it be an intriguing novel approach to an old problem, a repurposed solution from another area of the business, or something novel entirely, represent ideas that have the potential for real impact - not just iterative continuous improvement. The step change will be important to early pitches and will help you secure those early wins you seek. It may be that you are able to bring increased clarity on a problem that was pre-existing that you can add value to with your skill set, or it could be an opportunity; something not previously acknowledged but has revolutionary potential.

Present a data driven or researched background to what you're pitching. Your pitch can start with insights not previously seen, using some analysis from within the organisation or outside it, that shines a spotlight on something overlooked. Including a data driven approach gives much more to your argument for some key players in your audience who operate squarely on data driven metrics. You can also run a desktop scenario planning exercise on the back of any data collected to project what could happen if the interventions you are requesting are adopted.

Be flexible, and open about the solutions. Understand your audience beforehand, so you know whether a complete solution presented on the day works better than a half solution that the group then collaborates to complete. Both approaches have their merits, so consider which suits your context. Being flexible about the solution includes the way it is resourced. Consider options of permanent staff, freelancers, contractors, outsourcing, and automation as relevant, evaluating each before deciding which to put forward.

Don't over commit on timelines. What takes three months in one organisation can take one month or six in others, depending on how the organisation is set up, so be cautious on this; link your timelines for delivery very carefully to your resourcing scenarios. As is famously said, never over commit and under deliver! There are so many unknowns still at this stage in terms of how the team responds to pressure, the systems, and structures in place to ensure that the load is manageable and other projects running concurrently. It's fundamental to not just have some assumptions going into your scenarios but running realistic ones so you have a better idea of what's achievable.

Predetermine what early signs of success can look like, or how this can be measured. If you find better ways to measure it going forward do those too but define simple metrics upfront that you will be able to obtain and manage data for in a simple way. They will need to be metrics that improve results not just for your area but demonstrate an improvement in other areas as well.

Be sure to include what your key stakeholder wants in the pitch. Not what you think they want, nor what you think they should want, but make it obvious and clear that you've considered what they want first. You absolutely need that early buy in. It's advisable to understand the interests of all relevant stakeholders (even the ones who may be competing with you for a budget) in order to come up with a pitch that wins. Profile your audience and understand what type of decision makers they are - I cover this in significantly more detail in my full course programme.

Establish external performance benchmarks where none exists, as much as reasonably possible. An external benchmark for a company achieving what you are aiming to achieve holds more weight than your word alone, no matter how good and, or, established you are. Get those early credibility markers working for you. If you've done an identical project somewhere else with comparable results, then by all means this is your stage.

A recommendation from my personal experience; **make your slide deck visual, and succinct, with a central idea** that you sell with great storytelling. Consider who's in the room, the type of story, anecdotes and metaphors that will resonate. Each successive slide should reinforce the central ideas or argument of your first slide.

CHAPTER 15

Better than average, not perfect

How to earn funding for your projects and innovations

❖ *Is it good enough to be good enough?*

At the risk of sounding like I'm pitching this at a pretty low bar, for most things you need to do at work, it's already exceptional to be better than average.

Read that again.

It's exceptional to be better than average.

Going a step further, if you can achieve average competency at most things and be exceptional at just a few strategic things, your career is made.

For the entrepreneurial and managerial amongst us, the better you get at outsourcing your average, the more exceptional your whole team is. This is what it means to be strength based.

I am yet to see a person for whom the next statement isn't true, **you will be much better at developing a natural strength than at developing a weakness.** It doesn't mean you cannot achieve mastery levels on both, but the sacrifice you make on building weaker abilities will be bigger pound for pound as compared to enhancing and extending a strength.

That said, some of us have strengths that don't fit neatly into one thing. Neurodiversity being what it is, people considered to be on the spectrum of autism and ADHD tend to have a varying array of ways that they look at the world and connect ideas.

They can be great at problem solving, creating new to the world innovations, all they need is a supportive environment through which to explore their talent without being judged for their differences.

I'm not medically diagnosed as neurodivergent, but ADHD fits me well. In many ways it's a superpower. I can dive deep into random subjects that interest me, make sense of what I've learnt, recombine that knowledge with something else and come up with something new, all without any sleep. One of my clients calls me the alchemist. I'm capable of cracking on with a month's work in two days if I put my mind to it, when I'm going through a hyperactive phase.

This ability makes my strengths that of connecting dots, forging relationships, creativity, managing change and leading diverse teams with an affinity for inclusive practices.

The flip side of this is that I can lose focus for weeks on end and can work to the point of exhaustion because I don't always regulate when I switch off. I'm an exceptional generalist! And any attempt to make me perfect at any single skill will be short-lived.

Perfection

"All of us as individuals bring our set of experiences, our ways of working, our ways of thinking which is great. It's that diversity of thought and experiences that drive innovation. That's awesome. However, as a leader, you need to find a way to harness what I call the messy!

All of those people are also motivated differently. And they have baggage of things that are going on in their life and how they show up every day. And so, I think, as that leader who's trying to get everybody around, you're carrying everybody's imperfections into it. And so, the job of the leader is to harness the messiness of the imperfections, to get to the maximum benefit. It's kind of like a coach of the sports team. I have all of these players that I've got to put them together in the best possible way, so that we all win as a team, not just my superstar but the whole team has to work together. And how *do I do that? How do I motivate that? And particularly, I, as the leader, have my own baggage so I have to actually challenge my thinking. I think it's a give and take, but it's a realisation that none of us are perfect. There's not one way to do things. We've got to change it up and be willing to be curious and rethink what I thought I knew. "*

Interview with Melissa Carson - Leadership Coach and Organisational Strategy Advisor on the Do What Matters Podcast.

I loved this conversation with Melissa, where we explored perfection and how it represents differently depending on your span of control. It's a great episode to dig into on the podcast *Do What Matters*.

Many of you take pride in your perfect execution of jobs. Steven Bartlett - Author and Founder of *Social Chain*, and one of 30 under 30, talks a great deal about his pursuit of perfection, that the little things matter in creating the perfect experience for the listeners of his podcast, The Diary of a CEO, which by the way is well worth a listen.

We all know that continuous work and iterations on the product or service that we have, has the potential to bring greater results with each successive effort and can help you to build something that's more compelling than others. The only question is at what cost?

I attended Steven's show - *The Diary of a CEO Live* in early 2022, and there he speaks about another side of this too. He amassed a great fortune early on his entrepreneurial life, from being a university drop out at nineteen to building a company that on its initial public offering was worth over 300 million. But he talks about that pursuit of money ("wait till I get my money b...t...h") and what it cost him in terms of relationships with his business partner, his own self-care, his love life. He mentioned that he kept thinking that: when he made 30 million, he would change, then it became when he made 50 million, then, okay, he'd change when he made it to 100 million.

If you are building something that's going to be *net-positive* for you, your teams, the community that supports you and the planet, I recommend you start now and not some distant time in the future; factor the long game into the present reality. Your parameters for measurement will need to expand. In today's world of subjective measures, perfection is an impossibility, as the boundaries are unknown.

The real problem that perfection can bring to some of us is in the language we use to describe it. It's the difference between seeing yourself as having failed vs seeing yourself as having fallen, or as being good enough. If you've fallen, you get up right? If it's good enough it's accepted right? So, what if we took that philosophy into our life and work?

What I look at as continuous improvement another may consider to be persistent failure. When you are delivering a service, there's no such thing as perfect, as that's a subjective concept to be viewed from the perspective of each individual customer.

It's similar for products for individual consumption. There are basic parameters you need to meet (safety, security, product life cycle management), but a consumer's enjoyment of that product depends on the use case. And the degree of variability that's possible among different consumers.

I will concede that if your work is to make drugs, design buildings, rocket ships, guns, and nuclear power plants; precision matters and checks and balances are worth paying extra for. For the rest of us, failure is opportunity.

What I recommend is that we strive toward accepting ourselves as organisms in constant growth.

- Acceptance is getting in touch with the present-day version of yourself. Past versions had experiences and lessons that brought you to this moment and today's *you* is capable of making informed judgements about present circumstances because of the accumulated lessons that went before.

- Acceptance to grow means that today you are deploying the best skills and tools you've accumulated over the years to solve this problem, no matter what happens tomorrow. The tool I find most useful in acceptance is the skill of journaling, and there's a mini podcast episode on this topic in Do What Matters – Career and Leadership on Purpose Podcast.

- Acceptance acknowledges that tomorrow's version of you will certainly make different decisions if you take an action that produces new insight and information today. What I mean by that: it is through our actions that we learn and improve our ability to respond appropriately to challenges. The next version of you tomorrow, will be smarter for any decisions you make today.

- Acceptance eliminates the language of failure and gives way to lessons, data, information, learning. It opens you up to understanding not just what you demand from yourself, but what others are interested in receiving from you as well.

Here's a new affirmation to try out: instead of *"I'll try to get this right today"*, think instead *"I'll improve yesterday's version of me today"*.

❖ *What's your exceptional magic, and how are you going about developing it?*

I've made the mistake during my corporate career to make my teams focus on their weaknesses and design their development plans around those. I now see the cost of such an approach, while at the time I thought there were only benefits. I didn't always keep perspective of the long view; else I'd have understood this even then. I may have extinguished some bright sparks with this antiquated approach to development.

It's probably the main reason corporate development plans work less well if you haven't been marked for greatness and mentored by a senior manager with genuine interest in your success, causing attrition from the system.

It is also a possible explanation for why I feel like all the entrepreneurs I know are people on the neurodiversity spectrum that have dropped out of the system; it's harder for us to do fitting in when our thought processes are so fundamentally different, and it's hard for us to be employees, as we feel that imposter syndrome when trying to be like everyone else, or like others expect.

To be better than average, the rules are to know your strengths and grow them, understand yourself deeply and cover the basics with your other responsibilities or outsource them so they don't become liabilities. No one is asking for perfection here. The key is to be strategic with your time management.

CHAPTER 16

Duds and Explosives

How to deal with a toxic boss or culture

"If someone says something really sh*tty to me or to one of my children, I'm hardwired to punch him in the face, but I don't do that. And so, I think we can address the hardwiring with mindfulness and critical thinking, but I will tell you, positive emotion requires more complex thinking. It requires reality checking of some of the emotional feelings that we're having. I can't scare you into joining me. I have to engage with you, cognitively in a thinking way to inspire you to join me."

> Brene Brown & Simon Sinek on the Podcast
> a bit of Optimism – Titled: The One With
> Brene Brown

I loved this conversation between Simon Sinek and Brene Brown. It might be the best podcast episode I've ever listened to for one main reason, these are two people who exemplify the way two people should discuss a disagreement, or differences in ideologies, values, or beliefs. I'm inspired by how self - aware they both are, and that comes across so effortlessly in this conversation where both trade thoughts and ideas and end with an increased level of mutual respect.

This beautiful dance of words is not our everyday reality, however. Most of us, me included, are still learning self-mastery, and let's face it, some of us are not even on that journey in the first place. So how do we navigate difficult conversations when things don't go according to our plan?

Things are going to go dark a bit

The dark triad is a collection of three interrelated, malevolent personality constructs: narcissism, psychopathy, and Machiavellianism. All of these traits can exist on their own, or all together in one person, and can certainly present challenges such as unethical, disruptive, and outright criminal behaviour at work. This is the worst-case scenario of the type of individual who could grace your office floor. I'm going to define all these character traits, then it's time to talk about gaslighting.

According to *Psychology Today*, Narcissism is characterised by a grandiose sense of self-importance, a lack of empathy for others, a need for excessive admiration and the belief that one is unique and deserving of special treatment. If you encounter someone who consistently exhibits these behaviours then see the link to the article in the references of this text, you may be dealing with a highly narcissistic individual.

Narcissists

Narcissists are great at drawing all the energy in the room toward them, having the impact of everyone pandering to their needs above their own, and above yours as well. You may even find yourself justifying their behaviours, instead of focussing on what you need to do to get your points across or get investment in your ideas.

There are a couple of potential ways for dealing with this personality type:

- Answer a game with a game. Decide definitively whether your project or proposal really requires you being individually recognised, or whether it simply needs to get done. If you want to get something done, then you may wish to allow the narcissistic personality to take credit. The key here is knowing when to fight and when to allow the other to believe the idea was theirs.

- An alternative approach is to set clear boundaries around yourself and the way you work. Healthy boundaries are a fundamental strategy to protect your mental health and well-being from all forms of tyranny, so I recommend pursuing this as a strategy as a matter of habit. More on how to do this later.

Psychopathy

Again, referencing *Psychology Today*, psychopathy is a condition characterised by the absence of empathy and the blunting of other affective states. They can be highly manipulative while appearing charming.

Psychopaths are likely perpetrators of gaslighting, or subtle forms of manipulation within the organisational context. I've personally experienced the feelings of self-doubt then betrayal when some individuals have committed these acts in the past. Before I understood psychopathy and gaslighting, I put the experience down to white men that don't want to see a black Caribbean woman rise to her full potential. The truth is though, it's most likely to be perpetrated by white men simply because there are mostly white men in leadership positions still even today in general, although times are changing.

Successful professionals have come to me because their work has been constantly undermined. They've walked away from situations not only doubting themselves, but having the entire room doubt them too. If you don't know it exists, it's hard to know it's happening to you. It undermines fairness, equity, and justice, and most importantly, getting things done that are for the greater good, in exchange for personal gain. It's like living in an episode of Game of Thrones, trapped in a wine barrel, and surrounded by dragons. Forgive the imagery.

I don't talk about these topics to scare you, I talk about them because they form part of the real world, and not everyone will be on the same path to enlightenment that you, my reader, are on.

Gaslighting usually emanates from an authority figure, but not always; it can come from peers, and direct reports too, as long as they are emboldened by the prevailing culture of the time.

❖ This is what it looks like:

- Vague negative feedback that plants doubt in the minds of listeners without specific examples.

- Unclear deliverables or shifting goalposts, with scope creep outside the victim's role.

- New demands without allocating sufficient time for execution.

- Comparing two workers who do very different jobs that require different skills in a way that favours a personal preference for one over the other, not able to be verified by merit.

- A relentless focus on calling out weaknesses without acknowledging the strengths.

- Constant requests for cosmetic re-work without constructive feedback.

- Alluding that the employee may not be telling the truth, without providing evidence, and even resisting that evidence be displayed.

- Playing on the organisational hierarchy to suppress the employee's voice.

- Creating unfounded doubt in the employee's abilities.

❖ *What to do if you are being gaslit:*

- Acknowledge it. First step to recovery.

- Look out for red flags in your own behaviour (*my boss means well* - Stockholm Syndrome is not uncommon.)

- Keep a journal and study the triggers for that person responding that way. Start anticipating them as the key is to disarm them before they fire.

- I'm going to say something you probably won't like, but my advice would be to pause "feeling" the situation and start asking questions. For example, when he acts out and says don't speak to his team, ask him questions like how would this be understood by the team? How would such an approach affect productivity? What if we agreed on a process that incorporates all departments instead? The key is to keep asking practical questions to take away some of his "control tendencies" and bring it back to a conversation about process, methods, efficiency, effectiveness. This keeps you as the progressive and puts a defensive posture back on them. Questions are your friend! I'd recommend you sit and write down different types of questions you would ask in all of those scenarios. It's your most powerful defence against gaslighting.

- Sit with yourself for a while and ask yourself where you may be feeling insecure about somethings, as gas lighters tap into your own insecurities. The key would be to identify the insecurities, and work to close them, and even to design questions around them if they are knowledge based so again you disarm the firing gun.

- Prepare for an open and honest conversation with the offender if the situation has become out of hand. It's important to keep your cool, and steady your emotions, as they thrive on creating that emotional havoc.

Machiavellianism

From Science direct: Machiavellianism is associated with the doctrine of moral expediency and deviousness in political actions; the divorce of politics from private morality; and the justification of all political means, even the most unscrupulous when the interests of the state (or perhaps the organisation or department) are at stake.

Unlike the other two traits we discussed before, this one may be the greatest hindrance to inclusive and *net-positive* leadership, because it's typically not anchored in the greater good for all but takes a limited context of protecting a defined domain.

That said, this can also become a morally subjective positive trait that helps re-define laws that are no longer fit for purpose, especially when the actor has the good of the people and the planet in mind. It's the kind of trait we may see in heroes - Jon Snow and Daenerys Targaryen spring to mind in the last season of Game of Thrones (no spoilers).

What about the Duds?

There's a little talk about workplace character that for the purposes of this text I'm calling the dud. This is someone who has power in the organisation from tenure and title but behaves powerlessly in the face of adversity. They seldom step up to defend their team and are a bit like the runt of the litter in the decision-making forums, only getting the scraps on budget and every other resource allocation. This character becomes especially problematic when they are your boss.

We will encounter managers in our lifetime who do not have leadership training, or who have been thrust into positions of leadership without the desire to lead. Sometimes they are excellent technicians and have exceptional skills beyond the average of the organisation on some critical aspects of the role, but in reality, they either should not be leading teams (because they have no desire to acquire team leadership skills) or they need a programme of training.

When working with these characters there's something really important to acknowledge; they do listen to others and accept the authority of others. Some may have a profile where they are not receptive to feedback from their team, but most, if you create the right environment for the conversation, will listen to your feedback on how their performance impacts the team. Come to that session with short-, medium- and long-term solutions. As these individuals likely need training, things will not change quickly, so a short-term solution would be that you show up where decisions are being made and advocate for yourself.

Where this open and honest conversation doesn't work, I recommend looking to this individual's peers or line manager, to gain advanced support for the pitch or change mission you want to implement in the organisation.

There is an increased demand on you as an employee when your boss does not demonstrate the capability to support your work. Where organisations transparently perform 360-degree feedback, these issues can be more easily handled, but the onus will always be on the employee, to find a way within the rules and ethics of the game to have your ideas and solutions considered.

Duds can become launch pads for a greater career for you, as you will, by necessity, begin managing and leading up. The worst thing you can do is lead the way the dud does, by not speaking up and not acting where action is indeed required.

Boundaries are your friend

Recently I worked with a phenomenal friend. She exhibits traits of ADHD and Autism, and her two boys also have Autism. Her journey to raise her sons and discover these characteristics about herself are nothing short of inspiring to me, and to this day she has written the best work I've ever seen on boundaries.

One of the central ideas I learned from her work was this idea of consent. As humans, we need to establish parameters by which consent must be given before a course of action that impacts me is followed. It's a concept that wouldn't thrive well in autocratic, bureaucratic, and hierarchical organisations, but if it did, it seems clear to me that attempts at inclusion would succeed.

If you want to establish clear boundaries at work, consider the types of areas for which you believe you must give consent.

Once you've established these, practise with peers and then make a formal statement to the meeting where this behaviour typically happens, or in other relevant settings about your boundaries and why they are needed. This is an employee rights issue, but in approaching it in this way, you may find you get considerable buy-in from others dealing with similar situations.

Consider discussing these topics with HR, to update your employee handbook and or meeting charters to include this fundamental idea of consent on interactions.

The Role of Culture

What is culture - especially as we move into a hybrid digital and remote, and office-based environment? Culture is often defined in the organisational context as the way the organisation works, and it comes with this idea of culture fit. In my view, culture fit is an outdated concept that does not belong in the modern, inclusive, and *net-positive* organisation. Instead, organisational culture should be an ideal on how the organisation interacts with each other. The difference? We do not reject candidates who do not fit the culture. We hire and hold the culture statement up as a standard that we are all working toward.

Instead of using it as some form of yardstick, it should be used to drive continuous professional development of teams and individuals who are struggling to use language, communicate in ways that consider their audience meaningfully and seek consent first.

We often acknowledge the importance of a culture in driving an outcome, yet many older organisations fall into a culture trap, because the old culture no longer fits the new world, and the transition to the new takes longer as the organisation's memory is long and takes time to fade.

The primary role of your culture is to:

- Create psychological safety for team members to do their best work toward the organisation's goals.

- Inspire innovation, continuous improvement, and an appetite for lifelong learning.

- Inspire collaboration, curiosity, creativity, and problem solving among its communities.

Does your organisation's culture live up to the ideal?

Dealing with Fear and Anxiety

When dealing with toxic people, we need to get a hold of our own deep-seated insecurities and fears, so I thought I'd cover this here.

Fear and anxiety are factors of both nature and nurture. I am by no means a mental health expert, and if you suffer from chronic anxiety, I absolutely recommend seeking mental health support with a recognised therapist. If, however, you want a nurture approach to help relieve some of the fear and anxious tension, then consider reading on.

If we are living with fear and anxiety without dealing with it, we incubate it every day of our lives, making those feelings only grow, until it has disabled us. I know what I'm talking about from personal experience. I have two simultaneous relationships with fear and anxiety. Mentally, I trust myself to make good decisions, come up with fresh ideas, develop solutions on the fly, so I'm typically not afraid to sound stupid in meetings; I will speak up without hesitation. In virtual meetings I have no problem presenting confidently the way in which I process my world, and this comes across to my clients.

If you put me in the same situation and ask me to do the same things in person physically, you will see a different me. One that is way shyer and more retreating. This is due to body dysmorphia anxiety that I still carry. This is a force so well incubated in me, especially since the pandemic and all the time I've spent at home, it sees me cancelling social events and generally retreating from being out in public. I have created a habit of fear, anxiety, and retreat to safety where my body is concerned, but where my pen, my words or my voice is concerned, I have developed a strength.

Both of these behaviours happen because of the thoughts I harbour and nurture; twenty years ago, my voice was less developed, but I was physically less fearful.

My point is, for some of us, fear or anxiety is something we nurture in the place of bravery, courage, and exhilarated energy.

In 2019 I set myself two physical challenges to help me create a pattern interrupt in my life around my athletic confidence and body dysmorphia. I decided to bungee jump from a tower in Auckland and two days later I did a hike across the Tongariro Crossing in the centre of the North Island of New Zealand; the area where they filmed the Mordor scenes in the Lord of the Rings. Both were extreme physical challenges that I didn't know I could do. For both, I felt chronic fear before I did them. For both, I embraced bravery and courage to take my first step. For both, I felt exhilarated at the end.

❖ Imposter syndrome can be reduced by taking action.

Success triggers fear and imposter syndrome to flare up, because we think the law of averages means that at some point, we are going to fail at this eventually, and every success brings us closer to a bigger and bigger failure, and causes us to, at times, self-sabotage because we fear failing later on. It's as if it's not acceptable for us to simply enjoy the present and the journey, we constantly scan the future for signs of peril and try to get ahead of it in a way that makes us feel a false sense of safety. In truth, by slinking back into a comfort zone, we prolong a practice of deriding ourselves into being less than our potential.

Fear and retreat blocks curiosity and experimentation. We are less likely to explore ourselves and the depth of our capabilities when we feel fear. As we need to train our muscles with stretching, yoga, and exercise, we need to train our mind with challenges of different complexities.

Fear fires up defences, and defensive people internalise, instead of considering shared responsibilities, or even exploring the topic in more depth.

Comparison is our other Achilles heel. Constant comparison can bring about judgement if we view the world through a filter of "people are either worse than me, or better than me". Once this judgement and ranking system is at work in our minds, it's hard to remove. This is something I believe our school systems nurture with test score rankings and the like, and sporting competitions also support this idea.

It may be that the 100th ranked tennis player in the world feels badly about their achievements relative to other tennis players, yet the reality is, they are the 100th best tennis player in their category in the world – and in a world of 7 billion plus, that is overachieving!

Once you begin to entertain thoughts that you aren't good enough, then you find evidence to support that you aren't good enough. What if you considered it the other way around - and started looking for justifications for why you are good enough?

My point is wherever possible, we must consider the potential of using our minds to reinforce positive behaviours we want in our own lives, relationships, and businesses, instead of the opposite, as this is far more likely to develop into short-, medium- and long-term gain, than spending our time ruminating on all that is negative.

The key to managing fear and anxiety is to rebrand those feelings with new labels or flip their use cases to their positive alternatives. Words matter. If you say failure, it means something different than saying I've fallen. Fallen people get back up for example. If you say I don't know enough, and leave it at that, you may stop trying. If you say I don't know enough yet, that then suggests that there is room for growth.

The tone you use in your own self talk also matters. You must have heard about Amy Cuddy's famous TED talk in which she talks about power posing and increasing hormones that foster more boldness and bravery in you. Our chemical makeup is a fascinating minefield of discovery; and ways to naturally increase the flow of certain hormones in our bodies is a key pathway to helping us overcome what suppresses us. If we relate our language with self and others through the use of more positive and empowering words, our trajectory to the future can be quite different.

The word *fear* usually hangs out with the words doubt, failure and frustration. How about if we associated the word, where reasonable, with words like energy, excitement, and growth?

❖ *Fear is triggered*

We have, over time, accumulated trigger stimuli and responses that invoke fear when experienced. Some of these are useful. When you hear a car horn or the rumbling of a city bus behind you while cycling, you hold your line and alert yourself to hyper vigilance in case of risk. There are still other fear-triggered responses that are less useful.

For example, an introvert, being introduced to a group of new people. It's a terrifying experience for introverts, as a lot of noise is taking place in our minds. What will they think of me? What if I don't remember their names? Will they want to talk to me after? I prefer to retreat where it's safe. Here we have a flight or fight response being triggered, where I would argue in all of our experiences, we've never been attacked by someone we've just been introduced to. A more helpful approach if you cannot avoid these situations may be to focus on just one person, or ready yourself beforehand with a few prompts of responses.

The action is to recognise the trigger and train yourself to have a new response, that leaves you feeling better after the encounter, not worse or the same. If your trigger is speaking in public, then make speaking in public a subject to study. Treat it like a science; something methodical you can learn.

Use your fear to drive acknowledgement, recognition, and action.

❖ Fear means growth

If you are not feeling fear, you've been in one place for too long. This applies to all of life. Feeling fear means you're moving beyond your comfort zone. Repeated action that pushes through those fear barriers, expands your comfort zone in the same way that stretching, and exercising expands your physical range. It is also possible to overdo it, so chunk your actions into mini and daily steps. Treat fear as a signal that you are about to become an even greater person.

CHAPTER 17

Support for your Journey

How to know if coaching or related services are right for you

The leader needs a guide.

As your leadership responsibility grows, so does your risk of not achieving your goals. Heads of function and managers and change leaders today face unique challenges from many fronts:

- Income inequality and resource scarcity is having the impact of reversing the middle class in western countries and creating the environment for greater political instability.

- Wars over scarce resources are becoming more likely.

- New digital economies are emerging while climate change and the planetary boundaries continue to be breached.

- Changes in interpersonal relationships at home and at work as a result of the increased use of digital solutions to communicate and work.

- Increased potential for stranded assets as we move away from linear models to circular ones.

- Digital disruptors to the way your business is done, that are capable every few months of doing things, faster, better, and more sustainably.

- A workforce impacted by higher levels of physical ill health, and lack of mental wellbeing.

- An unsettled geopolitical landscape.

- The risk that as the ice sheets melt, we are faced with rising sea levels and exposure to once rare or dormant viruses.

- An increased cry for social justice and equality at work, that requires significant efforts in change management.

Many leaders are using this time of great transition for a great reset. Senior leaders seeking growth are drawing on the services of coaching to help them make some critical adjustments to face what's ahead. It's helpful to understand a few key principles about coaching and related services such as mentorship and therapy.

The coaching industry is massive and continues to grow. The growth is also making its principles more accessible to everyone.

In 2002 when I had my first coaching experience, it was limited to a group of about twelve employees across my organisation, but today you can procure the services of a coach yourself to help you grow.

As the industry swells, services are becoming more niched and nuanced. My coaching lens is to support career transitions and start-ups, with the principles of sustainable business leadership infused in my work. Other coaches will have other filters to help you improve some specific aspect of your overall well-being.

I collaborate in my coaching courses and programmes with mindset specialists, HR professionals and business leaders to bring views that stretch beyond the strict remits of coaching. This helps during career transitioning as there's a large part of this process that's about building confidence in something new and unknown.

In 2018, I had a transition plan for my life that I worked with a coach to help me execute. We met once a month and between sessions I did the work to fill in the blanks. I loved the process and the journey so much that when our relationship ended naturally as I had moved on to what was next, I decided to become a student of coaching in a formal way, choosing the Pegasus NLP school in the New Forest to learn the trade from a psychotherapist with more than 40 years' experience.

The group was about fourteen people, with a fair mix between employees learning the skills to become better coaches and leaders at work, to entrepreneurs learning the skills to become private coaches. These skills should be mandatory in schools of all levels; especially as we work to transform the BAU of a broken capitalism to something more inclusive to all.

If coaching is something you are considering, then I ought to give you some advice on how to go about it.

How to choose a coach, mentor and or therapist

The first thing to learn is that these are not the same disciplines.

I've had the need to utilise all of these services in my career both in business and as an entrepreneur, and they are all relevant and fundamental to creating important breakthroughs with their clients.

One person can possess all three skills, but this is hardly recommended as the skills are administered differently for a reason.

❖ Mentors

A mentor has done something you are trying to do before you. The mentor is practical, with useful advice specific to your circumstance, typically on things you can't easily learn in a textbook. They are knowledgeable, influential and use storytelling to sell ideas and methods, they're usually strongly opinionated on whatever the topic you wish to learn more about.

Mentors are great for:

- Building networks/ introductions.
- Organisational politics.

- Passing on Tacit knowledge.

- Discipline specific knowledge.

Mentors are less useful when:

- Assumptions are changing.

- They are no longer in the game.

- Their ideals and values are too different from your own.

A mentor helps you fast track your learning, but I don't recommend one mentor for all of your career, have specific ones for identified topics and change them up from time to time. This is usually an unpaid service for people within organisations, but for freelancers, entrepreneurs and contractors, paid relationships are not uncommon particularly where they support business development.

Reverse mentoring is designed to remediate some of the weaknesses of mentoring, where the mentee actually brings useful insights to the mentor. It's particularly useful today, with the rapid pace of change and it leads to a more collegial relationship.

❖ Coaches

A coach leverages specific tools and patterns to disrupt your thinking and broaden your perspectives, with a view to helping you achieve self-mastery.

The coach works like a mirror, reflecting the coaching client's thoughts back to them, so the client can see patterns, behaviours, habits, and routines that may be hindering or harming them.

Coaches help with:

- Self-Awareness.

- General sensing and interpreting of your environment.

- Developing the skill of great questioning.

- Supporting you to create shifts and behavioural changes.

They are less helpful when:

- The coachee has unresolved past trauma that blocks forward momentum.

- There is a mismatch in terms of the support you need and what they can provide.

Coaches are a brilliant resource to create momentum toward a goal and are exceptional at embedding a growth mindset. A coach often isn't a full solution. In sport, tennis players travel with mindset coaches, technical coaches, physical coaches.

❖ Therapy

Therapy is healing past trauma. It takes time, but is crucial to breaking the old or deeply ingrained hurts to allow light in.

Therapists help with:

- Healing trauma.
- Creating safety.
- Remediating triggers.

Therapists are not great for:

- Solving external problems.

- Helping you build toward goals that are outside of the healing journey.

If something keeps coming up and blocking your path in every relationship, definitely get a therapist.

It's pretty archaic to think that needing therapy means you're crazy, or that getting support with your mental health is a sign of weakness. In fact, it's become the opposite; in leading societies, mental wellness is highly regarded and encouraged.

Your car lasts longer when you take it for regular check-ups and maintain it in good working order. Your body works best when you nourish it with healthy food, rest, exercise, and regular check-ups. Your brain works better when you also feed it with the stimulation, rest, and recovery it needs, and working with a relevant professional supports the journey.

Epilogue

The Aligned Mission

How to know if coaching or related services are right for you

❖ *Taking net-positive action - Get your GRIPP*

T he ultimate question every time has to be **Does my work help or harm the planet and or society as a whole?**

My mission in writing this book was to offer you an *Aligned approach to tacking complexity in a way that isn't intimidating, yet on purpose* and intentional. You have choices, make them with intention.

I have presented different ideas, science, and critical inflection points from my own life. I hope that I have helped to raise your consciousness to make better and more aligned decisions, anticipating things at every horizon.

I have already said it, but it is worthy of a reprise - *All the money in the world left for your children without a planet to live on does nothing to help anyone.* If you want to give your children every privilege, then let them join the sustainability mission. Train them to become problem solvers, change makers. *Net-positive* influencers. Give them more options than you've given yourselves.

Give them this book when they're choosing a career or path to follow.

I'd like to summarise the books lessons for leaders into a memorable mnemonic which I call the GRIPPS method. Spend your time on efforts that deliver on **G**rowth, **R**epeatability, **I**nsight, **P**romotability Psychology and **S**calability.

❖ *(Net-positive) Growth*

Growth is all about learning and the mindset that sets you apart as a leader building a *net-positive* workplace. It is about transforming your inner world toward curiosity, discovery, innovation, and implementation such that the system you are working within becomes more future fit, taking into consideration the emerging challenges.

❖ *Repeatability*

Repeatability is about those habits, mental models and mindset shifts you make that underscore how you consistently deliver on your goals.

It's having command of your playbook and mastery of your self-discipline and conscious processes, while nurturing your complete wellbeing. It's about resilience, sustainability for the self and about codifying your own methods to leverage them for future growth.

Be clear about which aspects of your playbook need repeating. Be mindful of your inbuilt biases as this can cause you to collect biased data points. Know intimately your outcome wheel and how that evolves over time.

❖ *Insight*

Creating value is increasingly a challenge of intellect and engineering. Our economies have thrived on extraction and conversion of value from the earth in a linear way, such that its use and re-use isn't repeatable - breaching the principles of *net-positive* growth. Today we must make every effort to use technology to advance the ideas of regeneration and renewables, circular business models, and digital experiences and, perhaps, pursuing further scientific experiments on the moon and mars to support extending the life of our planet.

It's not as economists report it - "de-growth", it's going to be more about optimising everything and letting nothing at all go to waste. It's a good challenge if we embrace it that way. We can continue to raise the living standards of everyone, with a bit of determined action to become more integrated with nature.

❖ Psychology and Promotability

Psychology and Promotability is about influence - managed in a *net-positive* way. Purpose isn't just a passing fad anymore, as more people young and old look for greater meaning from their day-to-day endeavours, purchases, and local contexts. Being able to promote the way we can make a difference will be essential going forward, as well as taking others along for the journey.

❖ Scalability

Solutions that scale well can be delivered at more affordable prices, and still present opportunities for profitability. This can be internally focussed on the self - improving your own ways of working, or on the organisation. It's mastery of systems, data, and information at scale.

❖ Mission Accomplished?

As I have shown throughout this book, we can all takes steps to get **GRIPPS** and in doing so live a purpose driven and *net-positive* working life, making informed, aligned, and considered choices.

Linked to this book I've created a number of workbooks to help you walk through the process and journey accompanied with guides and prompts from my experiences of leading others through this maze.

I also work with small group settings three times a year. Every January, May, and September, I run a three-month intense group career coaching course that supports you in living the principles in this book. Participants receive twelve group sessions plus two one-to-one coaching sessions of 60 minutes.

You also receive lifetime alumni access and an invitation to join workshops and learning sessions with subsequent cohorts where you need a refresher, or I have new insights to share. This includes close access to specially invited guests.

I also work one to one with business leaders, freelancers, contractors, and consultants on getting started and set up for success, or on course-correcting when things have gone off the rails.

For this I have 3-, 6- and 12-month packages of one-to-one support.

Apply the coupon code DO-WHAT-MATTERS to any of my one to one or group coaching services and get 20% off the price from 1ˢᵗ September 2022 until 30ᵗʰ April 2023.

Do What Matters **– The Career and Leadership on Purpose Podcast**

Also linked to this book is the brilliant podcast *Do what Matters*, released in June 2022 with a collection of interviews with people whose career pivots have inspired me.

You can find it on your favourite podcast host, or access episode transcripts www.katherineannbyam.com

I encourage you to reach out and connect with me on LinkedIn, the platform on which I spend most of my time generating more long form content that supports my views on things such as sustainable transitions and career development, search for Katherine Ann Byam, or use this URL here https://www.linkedin.com/in/katherinebyam/

If your path takes you deeper into sustainability, tune into The Sustainable Innovation Podcast - Where Ideas Launch for more Insight. You can find that on your favourite podcast hosting provider or access via the dedicated website here www.whereideaslaunch.com

I'm also on Instagram @katherineannbyam or @whereideaslaunch - happy to connect with you!

Reach out to me by DM on any of the socials above.

Thank you!

What's Next in the Series

This book series is the first in the Do What Matters – Pivot to Purpose Series.

This book has been written to act as a guide for readers throughout their lifetimes on making successful transitions and pivots, but I know it's not all that you need. Reach out to me on socials and find out how to join the courageous career club and become a lifetime member.

There are other topics I'm called to write about in subsequent books.

I've touched very briefly on topics of inclusion, but it's important enough to warrant its own dedicated text in this move toward more conscious *net-positive* leadership. I will be exploring DEI, Green Entrepreneurship, and something more personal, relationships over the next two-three years.

Here's an introduction to the future work to come.

Designed by Diversity, Built by Inclusion

I will likely never know how much of my life and career has been impacted by bias and privilege; what I do know is that I have, in the past, and continue to experience both, and that my character is stronger because of it.

The facts: bias is a feature not a bug. It's our brains' way of making us more responsive in decision making particularly when our immediate safety is concerned. It can however be weaponised against a minority group for arbitrary reasons, and I have been both victim and recipient of its privilege.

From this perspective, the first challenge is to understand your own bias. What are the models you're using to make decisions? How can you employ a healthy curiosity to find out if your assumptions are valid or invalid?

Biases become problematic when we don't pause to question or validate whether our biases are helpful or harmful to us and those around us.

This book will be a more personal journey, as well as lessons on why I consider that my life has been designed by diversity but built by inclusion. I'm looking forward to publishing this work in 2023/ 2024

The Purposeful Path - The Entrepreneur's guide to impact and income.

This book is about addressing the problem of *How do we do business better?* Not just taking a net-zero box without substance behind it, without considering the social side of the story.

When I started, I considered that there was no resource where I could find the complete big picture of how to land firmly on my feet, as a sustainable business-minded person with a deep connection to ethics. There are pockets of information for sure, specialisations in one domain of one area of the job, or another, but the experience of being an entrepreneur is not specialised or siloed and the challenges of being sustainable and conscious throughout your offer and your operations requires systemic and more integrated thinking.

Most entrepreneurs start solo or with a small team and have jobs with multiple facets. To be successful, you need enough exposure across all the various aspects of the business that you're building, so that you can be prepared for the relentless stream of decisions you need to constantly make.

Decision fatigue is absolutely real. In particular, when operating from a place of low trust. Low trust happens when brands, suppliers and service providers greenwash what they are doing. We don't want to be caught up in greenwashing If we are working hard to build an ethical reputation. Yet we are also faced with the challenge that much of the world's resources and means are accruing to businesses that don't share our views or are only now coming around to thinking about it. How do we build a space for collaboration and shared action?

When I understood what this journey was going to be like, I began to prepare a manual to walk with me as I step through all the hurdles along the way. I wanted to solve the problem of where to start, and what to consider for the millions of people who want to make a positive impact but are overwhelmed by all the things that just come up. I wanted to create signposts to great resources, templates, maps, and a navigation system to find the triple bottom line that's good for the planet, good for the people, and let's face it, what you need in your pocket.

You're likely a specialist in an area, and you want to trade either a service or a product, or software as a service, perhaps in your zone of genius, while having a *net-positive* impact on the world around you to round it off.

If you intend to start as an entrepreneur, get prepared to be uncomfortable in your first six months, as you figure out the market, consumers, their behaviours and how to serve them better. More often than not, the product you start with is not the one that will make you ultimately successful. You also need to be prepared to pivot and reshape your offer as many times as needed for as long as it takes. I'm starting with the fundamentals and building forward from there.

This book is going to be the Social Entrepreneur's Guidebook to doing what matters in business. I will go into the ways that impact driven entrepreneurs can thrive in business. Expect this book in 2022/2023.

The Naked Finger - A single woman's journey to find herself and her passion

In 2008 I wrote my first short story, about a trip to the Dominican Republic where I met a guy. My colleagues loved it because it was infused with a raw and healthy dose of self-deprecating humour.

They liked it so much in fact that I started writing regularly during all my international assignments, sharing my perspective on life on the road, & my journey to navigate culture.

Some of my best stories came from unusual places - Uzbekistan, Uganda.

They weren't meant to be stories about relationships, but my reflections as a single woman doing a job with a high level of international travel, relationships always got interesting and at times tricky to navigate.

In 2009 I moved to the UK. At first, I was impressed by every little detail. I felt a bit like an ant in a sea of different ant tribes marching off to do the day's work, but I was also fascinated by the level of diversity - of looks, language, and sense of personal freedom.

I arrived in May during peak summertime, and I couldn't believe I could go to work for long hours and still experience sunshine for hours at the end of the day; coming from Trinidad and Tobago, your daylight hours are pretty set - 6am to 6pm.

The honeymoon ended in January 2010, when the sky was pretty much at its darkest. I was completely depressed.

January is my birth month. In Trinidad and Tobago, it's not only warm, but we are usually warming up for our carnival road show, with parties and events every weekend! I couldn't adjust to the idea that no one seemed happy in the UK in January.

It got so bad I saw a therapist. In my talks with her, it came up that I was working on a book project, and she recommended that I put my energies into that, as a salve for the anxious feelings I was having. I didn't know then, but I was building a really useful habit of journaling and narrating my own life, and interrogating myself constantly, toward my own self-mastery.

This was my first ever book, and it will be the last I release. It's a story of my life in relationships and culture, and how it helped me step into my authentic self. My finger is still naked, without a wedding ring, but I'm pleased to share that I've been in a committed relationship for more than 11 years, and I've been working on this book for just over 13 years. It will be released in 2024/2025.

References

My reference list is a bit unconventional. I decided to highlight the top ten things that have helped mould and shape my thinking. You will find the topics of each varied and interesting, and seemingly unrelated.

My theory is this. When you appreciate some of the base principles in this book, you will be able to extract a meaningful lesson from every interaction, even if you're interacting with something or someone that does not share your values. I recommend interacting widely and with as much variety as possible with different people, content, interests. This is how you develop critical thinking skills that can help you and the planet to thrive.

If you own a physical copy of this book, visit my website www.katherineannbyam.com for hyperlinks to all resources.

The First 10 Episodes of Do What Matters

Do What Matters, The Career and Leadership on Purpose Podcast is available now on Apple, Spotify, and your regular podcast player, or on my website www.katherineannbyam.com

1. Katherine Ann Byam - Do What Matters

2. Shane Ward - The Purposeful Pivot

3. Tessa Clarke - Share more Waste less with Olio

4. Sherika Sherard - Busking through Vulnerability

5. Kysha Gibson - DEI is my Job

6. Katherine Ann Byam - Journaling

7. Melissa Carson - Leader's aren't Perfect

8. Katherine Ann Byam - Productivity

9. Juan-Luis Betancourt – Humantelligence

10. Katherine Ann Byam – LinkedIn

The Top 10 Episodes of Where Ideas Launch

Where Ideas Launch - The Sustainable Innovation Podcast is my first and internationally acclaimed podcast with some ground-breaking interviews. Tune in on your favourite podcast player, or via the website www.whereideaslaunch.com. Check out the episodes below.

F – Purpose driven Corporate Careers Learning Path – Where Ideas Launch

072 Transition Engineering – Where Ideas Launch

070 Growing A Successful ESG Consulting Practice[OBJ] – Where Ideas Launch

067 Systemic and Sustainable Mobility – Where Ideas Launch

055 – Green Finance – Where Ideas Launch

030 Future Talent – Where Ideas Launch

029 Feeding the World – Where Ideas Launch

027 + 028 Human Potential – Where Ideas Launch

026 Future Capital – Where Ideas Launch

019 The Knowledge Delusion – Where Ideas Launch

010 Leverage Your Strengths for Social Good – Where Ideas Launch

The Top 10 books that inspired this work

1. Doughnut Economics - Kate Raworth

2. Net Positive - Andrew Winston and Paul Polman

3. Atomic Habits - James Clear

4. Thinking Fast and Slow - Daniel Kahneman

5. Flow: The Psychology of Optimal Experience, Mihaly Csikszentmihalyi

6. The First 90 Days - Michael Watkins

7. Homodeus - Yuval Noah Harari

8. Tools and Weapons - Brad Smith

9. Surveillance Capitalism - Shoshana Zuboff

10. Human Compatible - Stuart Russell

The Top 10 movies that form part of the inspiration for this work.

1. An inconvenient truth

2. Living the Change

3. Breaking Boundaries

4. Seaspiracy

5. Cowspiracy

6. Saving Capitalism

7. Chasing Coral

8. Downfall - The case against Boeing

9. My Octopus Teacher

10. The Social Dilemma

The Top 10 TV series that form part of the inspiration for this work

1. Explained

2. How to become a tyrant

3. Human - The World Within

4. Dirty Money

5. Rotten

6. Lizzo - Watch out for the big Girrrls

7. Breaking Bad

8. Mad Men

9. Game of Thrones

10. Homeland

YouTube videos relevant to this work

1. Matthieu Ricard: How to let altruism be your guide

2. A healthy economy should be designed to thrive, not grow | Kate Raworth

3. 10 years to transform the future of humanity -- or destabilize the planet | Johan Rockström

4. The Anthropocene: Where on Earth are we Going? (Full)

5. Former Unilever CEO Paul Polman Says Aiming for Sustainability Isn't Enough. The Goal Is Much Higher

6. Net Positive, with Andrew Winston

7. A Life on Our Planet   David Attenborough

8. Naomi Klein: This Changes Everything live with Owen Jones - Full Length | Guardian Live

9. Earthshot Prize - YouTube

10. Cambridge Institute for Sustainability Leadership - YouTube

Websites referenced in this work

1. https://www.psychologytoday.com/us/blog/toxic-relationships/201812/how-spot-a Narcissist-

2. https://www.psychologytoday.com/us/basics/psychopathy

3. https://www.sciencedirect.com/topics/psychology/machiavellianism

4. This Is Exactly How You Should Train Yourself to Be Smarter [Infographic] | by Michael Simmons | Accelerated Intelligence | Medium

5. Best Articles: Over 100 Interesting Articles to Read (jamesclear.com)

6. Category: Shop - VIEW FROM MY WINDOW

7. THE 17 GOALS | Sustainable Development (un.org)

8. Ecology and Society: Planetary Boundaries: Exploring the Safe Operating Space for Humanity

9. Project Drawdown

10. Earth Overshoot Day 2022 home - #MoveTheDate

Quotes with Special Permissions

I have quoted works belonging to Simon Sinek and Simon Sinek Inc in this book. This work has not been officially endorsed by Simon Sinek or Simon Sinek Inc, but has been quoted with permission. To go deeper on his work, please refer to his website www.simonsinek.com. Brene Brown was also quoted as part of Simon Sinek's podcast. She has also given her permission with the warning that the rest of this work has not been endorsed by her.

I have quoted works belonging to Andrew Winston and Paul Polman in this book. This work has not been officially endorsed by them but has been quoted with permission. Permission is granted for non-exclusive rights to republish the quotes in both print and electronic formats, throughout the world in English Language. These credits apply where referenced:

"Net Positive" by Paul Polman and Andrew S. Winston. (c) 2021 Paul Polman and Andrew S. Winston. Republished by permission.

I have referenced the doughnut economics model by explanations, articulating an alternative view of economics, under the Creative Commons Attribution 4.0 International use license, duly crediting the author and the organisation.

Special permissions to reference messages and quotes have also been sought and received from the following people: Chris Pirie, Shane Ward, Anna Derinova-Hartmann, Susan Krumdieck, Melissa Carson, Ludwig May, Carlos Garcia, Archita Fritz, Kate Davis.

I have quoted works from Ecology and Society in this text, licensed under the Creative Commons Attribution 4.0 International use license. The article is duly referenced accordingly:

Rockström, J., W. Steffen, K. Noone, Å. Persson, F. S. Chapin, III, E. Lambin, T. M. Lenton, M. Scheffer, C. Folke, H. Schellnhuber, B. Nykvist, C. A. De Wit, T. Hughes, S. van der Leeuw, H. Rodhe, S. Sörlin, P. K. Snyder, R. Costanza, U. Svedin, M. Falkenmark, L. Karlberg, R. W. Corell, V. J. Fabry, J. Hansen, B. Walker, D. Liverman, K. Richardson, P. Crutzen, and J. Foley. 2009. Planetary boundaries:exploring the safe operating space for humanity. Ecology and Society 14(2): 32. [online] URL: http://www.ecologyandsociety.org/vol14/iss2/art32/

I have referenced the work of many others based on information in the public domain and have duly referenced them where appropriate under the fair use rule. This in no way suggests that this work has been endorsed by them.

Acknowledgements

Writing a book is a fascinating project with so many dimensions. Getting to the end of a project like this is incredibly rewarding, yet it is an exhausting process, and it's better when you have support.

I chose to self-publish, but I hired a vast team of freelancers to support me with various aspects of this project, and I want to acknowledge them all in order of engagement.

My book coach, Holly Hudson. She reached out to me in December 2021, as a ghost writer, offering me support to write my book. I had at that time been putting off getting started on it, but knew I had a lot to offer in this format, so I pulled the trigger. Holly didn't ghost write for me, but she did give me structure, helping me with the goals, the outline, and getting through the first phase of writing the manuscript with weekly calls, critical commentary, and interesting insights. Thank you, Holly, I couldn't get here without your support and guidance.

I'm a fan of supporting small businesses. One small business I love supporting is Trousseau Studios, run by Fanny Rousseau. Fanny is a slow fashion designer and graphic artist from France, who I've been collaborating with on various projects since the beginning of 2021. She brought my vision for the book cover to life and represented my personality wonderfully. Thank you, Fanny, for your ongoing support!

My editorial team is made up of 2 British English teachers. I'm a native speaker of Trinidad and Tobago's English and Trinidad and Tobago dialects – it's been immensely useful to have Harriet Pope and Louisa Herridge to realise the grammar and the structure. Louisa helped significantly with the flow of this book, and I'm very grateful!

I also hired someone for formatting from the app Fiverr for the first time. He goes by the name of Talha1280 from Pakistan, and he did a wonderful and meticulous job of lining everything up for KDP publishing. Thanks for your excellent work!

Featured guests and friends – Shane Ward has been a tremendous ally to have in this project, along with my friend Vinita Johnson. Together, they both gave me the perfect dose of tough love and critical insight to realise the product in your hands today. This would not be the great product it is without both of you.

To my marketing and PR team: Jay Rana, Melissa Hobson, Narrisa Mandol, Owen Sammarone, Myca Favorito, and the team at Ripple Impact – Thank you for the none stop support and advice throughout this process, and for all you will do to help in the future! Marketing a book is as much work as writing it, so really value your advice and encouragement, and active support on the process as well.

My early reviewers and other guest collaborators who I've quoted in the book – Thank you for your patience and continuous encouragement! Special thanks to Ludwig May, Melissa Carson, Felicio Ferraz, Anna Derinova-Hartmann, Carlos Garcia, Archita Fritz, Chris Pirie, Susan Krumdieck, and Kate Davis.

My Facebook, LinkedIn and Instagram communities who have been encouraging and egging me on throughout this process. Thank you for the amazing support!!

My family and friends, who have been cheering me on, and finally, my partner, without whose support I wouldn't be able to realise any of it.

Thank you!

About the Author

Katherine Ann Byam is an author, sustainability activist, coach and consultant for business resilience and sustainable change, partnering with leaders committed to a shared future for the planet. She's also Managing Director and CFO at Dieple Consulting.

A professional with 20+years change leadership experience in the FTSE Top 10, she pivoted to freelance consulting in 2019 to support sustainable development within SMEs.

Katherine holds an MBA with distinction, specialising in Innovation Management as well as certificates in ESG, digital strategy, and sustainability management from established universities. She's also a Fellow of the Association of Certified Chartered Accountants.

She's the host of the internationally acclaimed Where Ideas Launch - Sustainable Innovation Podcast, ranked among the top 5% globally, achieving the top spot in 5 countries, and the top 10 in 19 separate charts.

As a sought-after sustainable development coach, leadership advisor and keynote speaker, she facilitates workshops and learning sessions for communities within global brands such as Amazon, Women Tech Global, ACCA, Stryker, Speak Up, Mind Channel and more.

She loves spending her spare time in nature, walking the western and southern coasts of the UK, France, and Tobago, or on the Northern and eastern coasts of Trinidad.

Resources

If you are interested in taking your career transition forward with support, have a look at the resources available on my website, www.katherineannbyam.com.

These resources include:

- A personal inventory checklist

- A 9 Step Career Transition Template

- A Stakeholder mapping guide

- 3 workbooks for each of parts 1, 2 and 3 of this guide.

If you'd like to find out when my next live virtual workshop begins, sign up to my email list via the website.

Enjoy making your transition impactful!

Lots of Love,

Kathy

Printed in Great Britain
by Amazon

86380901R00159